GUIDE TO
CHRISTMAS

BORIS STARLING

© Haynes Publishing 2019
First published October 2019

A CIP Catalogue record for this book
is available from the British Library.

ISBN: 978 1 78521 661 9 (print)

Library of Congress control no. 2019942912

Published by Haynes Publishing,
Sparkford, Yeovil, Somerset BA22 7JJ
Tel: 01963 440635
Int. tel: +44 1963 440635
Website: www.haynes.com

Printed in Malaysia.

Series Editor: David Allsop.

CONTENTS

Christmas is so taken for granted that much of what makes it so, well, 'Christmassy' remains unknown. In this absence of certainty lies the bluffer's natural habitat.

COME ALL YE BLUFFERS

Welcome to *The Bluffer's Guide to Christmas*, or – if you're pressed for time – *The Bluffer's Guide to Xmas*. As any good bluffer knows, 'Xmas' is, religiously speaking, a perfectly valid word: the letter 'X' is a Greek abbreviation for 'Christ'. Technically, you can also refer to Xenings (when babies are dunked in fonts while their godparents stand around wondering where the Champagne is), Xendom (where all the Xians live) and the former Olympic 100m champion Linford Xie.

In these atomised times, Christmas is the one time of year when families are bound to get together and, for many families, once a year is quite enough. As Leo Tolstoy almost said in *Anna Karenina*: 'All happy families are alike. Every unhappy family is unhappy in its own way, and finds that it all kicks off by the time of the Queen's Speech, if not before.'

Christmas is so taken for granted, however, that much of what makes it so, well, 'Christmassy' remains unknown. In this absence of certainty lies the bluffer's natural habitat. The guiding principle of bluffing, and the *raison d'être* of the Bluffer's Guides (now entering their fifth decade of imparting instant wit and wisdom) is that a little knowledge is a desirable thing. Since that is all most of us are ever going to have anyway, we might as well get to know how to spread it thinly but effectively (like Marmite, or Gentleman's Relish, or Sandwich Spread, or indeed any other significant British contribution to world gastronomy, all of which are best applied sparingly).

Careful manipulation of some rudimentary facts will help you bluff your way through with a reasonable degree of nonchalance. This is especially important in these heady days of instant online information. When everyone has Google literally at their fingertips, failure to polish your bluffing techniques will leave you at a social and professional disadvantage.

This book is therefore not a 'How To' guide, but rather a 'How To Pretend You Know How To' guide. (There is a subtle distinction.) As our series strapline reads: 'It's not what you know, it's what they think you know.' This book gives the basics of Christmas: myths and facts about the Nativity story; the history of how the Christmas celebration evolved; Santa Claus and the physics of delivering so many presents; how to choose and decorate Christmas trees; Christmas cards and round-robin letters; Christmas carols and the stories behind some of the best-known ones; Christmas food and drink; Christmas in culture (films and music); giving, receiving and opening Christmas presents; the socio-economic ramifications of

Christmas; Christmas around the world; and a guide to surviving Christmas.

Careful manipulation of some rudimentary facts will help you bluff your way through with a reasonable degree of nonchalance.

So come in hard, drop some esoteric facts, make a few opaque allusions, and with any luck your interlocutors will think you have the kind of inside knowledge usually confined to the most erudite of historians. If in doubt, ask yourself: What would Bruce Willis – star of one of the most famous Christmas films of all do? (*see* page 82). He'd bluff hard. He'd bluff harder. And when all else failed, he'd bluff hard with a vengeance.

Be like Bruce.

Matthew's Gospel is all bling and international intrigue, while Luke's is the social realist one. Matthew is James Bond; Luke is Ken Loach.

THE NATIVITY STORY

FESTIVE TEASER:
According to the baffling carol known as 'The Twelve Days of Christmas' (*see* page 58), an unusual number of Christmas gifts were received by someone unknown from someone known only as 'True Love'. Casually pretending to do a swift mental calculation to arrive at the exact number of gifts received cumulatively over 12 days is bluffing on an heroic scale. (Answer on page 111.)

Meanwhile, the number of gifts received from True Love on the First Day of Christmas is one: a partridge in a pear tree.

GOSPEL TRUTHS

When it comes to the biblical narrative of the Nativity, the bluffer knows three things:

1. that the birth of Jesus is only mentioned in two of the four Gospels
2. which two Gospels these are (Matthew and Luke)

3. and the similarities and differences between their respective accounts.

Both Matthew and Luke agree that:
- Jesus was born in Bethlehem during the reign of King Herod the Great
- His mother Mary was married to a man named Joseph
- Joseph was descended from King David and was not Jesus's biological father
- Jesus's birth was a direct result of divine intervention.

Matthew's Gospel is the sole source for:
- The arrival of the Magi ('Wise Men') from the East bearing gold, frankincense and myrrh though (top bluffer fact) Matthew doesn't say how many Magi there actually are. The common figure of three comes purely from the fact that the visitors brought three gifts with them.[1]
- King Herod's massacre of the innocents, the order to kill all first-born children
- Mary and Joseph's flight to Egypt after being warned in a dream.

Luke's Gospel is the sole source for:
- The census which forces Joseph and Mary to go from Nazareth to Bethlehem

---

1 There could easily have been two Magi with a present each and arguing incessantly about who was going to hold the third; equally, there could have been a dozen Magi buckling under the weight of the enormous gold bar and jumbo-sized urn of frankincense they'd brought, because *someone* hadn't checked the item size before they hit 'Buy Now' on the Amazon website.

- There being no room at the inn (hardly surprising, to be fair: everywhere's booked solid at Christmas), meaning that Mary has to give birth in a stable and lay the baby Jesus in a manger[2]
- The shepherds watching their flocks by night who go to see the baby because an angel tells them to.

Basically, Matthew's Gospel is all bling and international intrigue, while Luke's is the social realist one. Matthew is James Bond; Luke is Ken Loach.

Most scholars assume that Jesus was born sometime between 6 BC and 4 BC: that is, between six and four years before himself.

YEAR ZERO

No one knows for sure exactly when the two Gospels were written or how much deliberate overlap there was between them,[3] but the scholarly consensus is that they were written independently of each other around AD 75–85. Neither Gospel gives a date for Jesus's birth, though the one thing that can be said with certainty

---

2 Not to be confused with Pret A Manger, whose campaign for domination of the global sandwich market was still a couple of millennia away.

3 Bringing to mind an image of the two men in an exam hall with one curling his arm protectively around his paper to stop the other from cribbing his work.

is that the traditional date – 25 December AD 1[4] – is nowhere near the actual date.

Using historical records (such as the death of Herod) and counting back from events in Jesus's own life, most scholars assume that Jesus was born sometime between 6 BC and 4 BC; that is, between six and four years before himself, which means either that the whole BC system is out, that the manger was also a time machine sending the baby Jesus a few years back to the future, or that like certain actresses Jesus lopped a few discreet years off his age for public consumption.

Whichever year it was, 25 December it wasn't. (The reasons behind it being chosen as Christmas Day are covered in the next chapter.) For a start, shepherds would have been unlikely to have still been in the fields in the depths of winter: snow around Jerusalem (only 10 miles from Bethlehem) was by no means unknown.

CENSUS CONSENSUS

Moreover, the Romans – ruthlessly efficient and organised as they were[5] – wouldn't have scheduled

---

4 Logically, perhaps, there should have been a year zero (as in AD 0, not as in Pol Pot's murderous attempts to restart Cambodia's calendar in the 1970s), but this logic is based only on the fact that we're used to years ending with '0'. Actually, not having a AD 0 is perfectly logical. AD stands for Anno Domini, 'Year of our Lord'. If 1 BC was the last year Before Christ, then AD 1 is the first Year of our Lord. There's no room for a zero here: the clock is ticking on year one from the moment Mary gives birth.

5 However did they turn into Italians?

a census for that time of the year, when weather conditions would have made travel difficult. Nor would they have scheduled one for the height of summer when, in a predominantly agrarian society, most people would have been involved in bringing in the harvest.

The most likely time for Jesus's birth would therefore probably have been after the harvest had been gathered in September or October,[6] which means that his *conception* could have been around 25 December. As for the Magi, even if Matthew gives them neither name nor number, history has filled in the gaps since then. 'Magi' is the plural of the Latin word 'magus', borrowed from the Greek 'magos', which is itself derived from the Old Persian word for the priestly caste of Zoroastrianism.[7] As such, they are as likely to have been riding horses as camels: by the time Jesus was born, camels were increasingly being used as pack animals, but Arabian horses were the transport choice for those who wanted to arrive in style. Definitely Premium Economy, if not actually First Class.[8]

The approximation of the translation to 'wise men'

---

6 The author was taught to drive by a man who, after lots of research and triangulation of star movements etc, had fixed Christmas as 16 September. He spent a lot of time telling me this when he should have been teaching me three-point turns and emergency stops. Lovely bloke, though.

7 The most famous recent adherent to Zoroastrianism was Freddie Mercury, who would surely have admired the glitziness of Matthew's account of the Magi.

8 At this point, the bluffer can, of course, drop in the old adage about a camel being a horse designed by a committee.

is therefore valid,[9] but not that to 'kings' in the strictly monarchical sense. This latter appellation is likely to come from Old Testament prophecies in Isaiah and Psalms which describe kings falling down and worshipping the Messiah. The Magi were therefore unlikely to be singing 'We Three Kings of Orient[10] are . . .' as they followed yonder star.

Western Christianity nowadays regards the Magi as saints. They're most commonly known as Caspar, Melchior and Balthazar.[11] In common with other tripartite sets, such as the Fates from Greek mythology, they're divided by generation as much as anything else: old man, middle-aged man, young man.

Caspar is the grandfather figure, often thought to have been from Tarsus (now in Turkey), and he brought the gold. Melchior is the middle one, and he brought frankincense (a perfume) from Arabia. Balthazar, who brought myrrh (an oil for anointing and embalming), is both the youngest and darkest-skinned, perhaps originally from as far south as Ethiopia. Gold, frankincense and myrrh were all gifts traditionally given to a king, and they also each had a spiritual meaning:

---

9 Also referenced in one of Gary Larson's funniest *Far Side* cartoons, where three very nervous-looking Magi have ended up in a remote bar and are being threatened by an unshaven bruiser in a vest. 'Oh yeah?' the bruiser's saying. 'More like the three wise *guys*, I'd say.'

10 Unless, of course, they were fans of east London football team Leyton Orient.

11 Modern-day Nativity scenes don't, of course, necessarily confine themselves to just the three Magi. In more contemporary constructs Darth Vader and Bob the Builder have both been seen manger-side, as it were, and indeed the Christ child has been obligated to share that manger with companions as diverse as velociraptors and scale-model Ferrari 488s (i.e. whatever the children helping to construct the scene have to hand).

- gold to represent kingship and virtue
- frankincense to represent deity and prayer
- myrrh to represent suffering and death.[12]

The bluffer will casually drop in reference to the historic Council of Chalcedon in AD 451, which decreed that Jesus was hypostatic.

The references to kingship and deity bring us on to prime bluffer territory: was Jesus a man or a God? The experienced and confident bluffer – that's you, or at least it should be once you've reached the end of this book – will at this juncture casually drop in reference to the historic Council of Chalcedon in AD 451, which decreed that Jesus was hypostatic, i.e. both fully human and fully divine, the two natures coexisting alongside each other.[13] Bluffing doesn't get much better than this.

---

12 Nowadays, of course, the frankincense and myrrh could be carried in clear containers of no more than 100 millilitres, and the gold would have to be declared as part of currency export regulations.

13 Alternative theories had included monophysitistic (only one nature, whether human or divine) and miaphysitistic (the two natures united as one). If you can remember these, let alone pronounce them (especially after a few Christmas Day sherries), please apply to Bluffers' HQ for a gold card and/or black belt (delete as applicable).

Saturnalia ran from 17 to 25 December and included banqueting, gift-giving, partying, and probably an old James Bond film at 4.45 on BBC 1.

CHRISTMAS PAST

> **ON the Second Day of Christmas, gifts received to date from True Love:**
>
> **two turtle doves,**
> **and two partridges in a pear tree.**

So, if Jesus wasn't born on 25 December, why is that day celebrated? Again, no one knows for sure, but the most likely theories are as follows:

- **Saturnalia:** The date was selected as a result of and a reaction to the ancient Roman festival of Saturnalia, which ran from 17 to 25 December and included banqueting, gift-giving, partying, and probably an old James Bond film at 4.45 on BBC 1. Saturnalia was held in honour of Saturn, god of agriculture, and usual social order was turned upside down during it: slaves became masters, peasants ruled the city, businesses, courts and schools were closed, parking attendants took the day

THE BLUFFER'S GUIDE TO CHRISTMAS

off, and citizens were immune from punishment. Everybody wore a *pileus*, the conical 'cap of liberty' which slaves received on their freedom, and donned bright clothes rather than the usual white togas or dresses. Choosing the date of Saturnalia's end would have demonstrated Christianity's contrast to and triumph over paganism.

- **Winter solstice:** 25 December is almost immediately after the winter solstice, which was itself celebrated by many ancient peoples (such as the Norse, who would burn large logs during the festival of Yule and feast until they burned out up to a fortnight later: hence, of course, the Yule Log. Most cattle had been slaughtered, most wine and beer had been fermented, which meant tons of grub and booze.) The days begin to lengthen again after 21 December, which Christians saw as representing the Light of Christ entering the world. For the same reason in reverse, the nativity of St John the Baptist was celebrated on 24 June, just after the summer solstice. As John said of Jesus: 'He must increase, I must decrease.'[14]

- **Conception:** The conception of Jesus was thought in some circles to have taken place round about the spring equinox in March, and/or that his crucifixion had taken place round about the same time in the calendar year too.[15] The latter is significant as some people believed that great prophets were conceived

---

14 Not a rejected Weight Watchers slogan.

15 Not in the same year, obviously, else we really are getting into causal time loops.

into the afterlife on the same date that they had been conceived into the world.

In the Middle Ages Christmas was a public festival at which 'misrule' – drunkenness, gambling, revelry and more – was common.

The first evidence of Christmas being celebrated on 25 December comes from about the year 350, when Pope Julius I declared that day as Christmas Day following work by Dionysius Exiguus, a Scythian monk who was an abbot in Rome. Cheers, Dionysius! The day itself received a boost when Charlemagne was crowned Holy Roman Emperor on 25 December 800, and at least two English kings, East Anglian monarch Edmund the Martyr and William the Conqueror, followed suit in 855 and 1066 respectively.[16]

MISRULE RULES

Christmas went from strength to strength in the Middle Ages. It was a public festival known as 'Christmas' (the first recorded use of the word itself dates from 1038)

---

16 Rulers had much better names back in the day. Among Charlemagne's successors were Louis the Pious, Charles the Bald and Charles the Fat: among other kings of English regions were Edgar the Peaceful, Sweyn Forkbeard, Harald Bluetooth (first monarch to use a hands-free mobile in his car) and of course Ethelred the Unready.

at which 'misrule' – drunkenness, gambling, revelry and more – was common.[17] Every year, someone lowly such as a beggar would be crowned Lord of Misrule, and would, with his celebrants, demand food and wine from the rich, threatening them with mischief if they didn't comply:[18] a brief, annual rebalancing of social inequality, if you like, and, of course, not a million miles from Saturnalia itself. Thus Christmas encompassed all strata of society. Richard II held a Christmas feast in 1377 at which 28 oxen and 300 sheep were eaten.[19]

CANCEL CHRISTMAS!

Elizabeth I liked to celebrate Christmas with dancing and sugar banquets, with elaborate sugar models – all edible, and all eaten – of pretty much anything you could think of: goblets, people, castles, dragons, and so on. Those twin sounds you can hear are a thousand dentists wincing in unison, and the glee of confectioners looking for a new *Game of Thrones* themed display.[20] By the 17th

---

17 Or, as we like to call it these days, Newcastle's Bigg Market on a Friday night.

18 Like modern-day Hallowe'en, basically. But with fewer Haribos.

19 Proving that the Atkins diet is by no means a new thing. And whatever happened to oxen? Have they all been eaten? Is Liverpool and England footballer Alex 'The Ox' Oxlade-Chamberlain the last recorded ox?

20 Elizabeth's teeth did actually turn black from eating too much sugar. She also carefully listed who'd given her what present and how much it had cost. (Presents in those days were given on New Year's Day.) The second part at least proves that Miranda Richardson's portrayal of her in *Blackadder* was not just screamingly funny but also an act of rare documentary fidelity.

century, Christmas had grown to feature masque balls and elaborate pageants too.

There was only one thing to do with all this fun. Ban it.

That's exactly what the Puritans did in 1647 following Parliament's victory over Charles I in the English Civil War.[21] This led, rather splendidly, to pro-Christmas rioting, with protestors in Canterbury breaking off from fighting to deck doorways with boughs of holly. Oliver Cromwell – 'Funtime Ollie', as no one ever called him – maintained the ban when he became Lord Protector in 1649 following Charles's execution.[22]

THE VICTORIAN EFFECT

Christmas was unbanned upon the restoration of the monarchy in 1660 but, rather like Sleazy Dave from university who always promised to reform and never quite did, it remained disreputable for some time afterwards. In Scotland, in fact, it wouldn't become an official public holiday again until … 1958! And if this wasn't shocking enough, Boxing Day didn't become a public holiday until 1974.

It wasn't until the Victorian era that Christmas

---

21 There was more to their decision than just antipathy towards revelry. Puritan preachers railed against Christmas as a Catholic invention, denouncing the 'trappings of popery' and the 'rags of the Beast'. It's quite hard not to say those phrases in an Ian Paisley accent.

22 Come to think of it, this may also be what inspired Alan Rickman's 'Cancel Christmas!' line in Robin Hood: Prince of Thieves. Not the first time Rickman had been involved in filmic Christmas shenanigans. See page 123.

began to morph into the festival we recognise as more or less the one we celebrate today. This drive came not just from the Anglican Church but also from writers such as Charles Dickens, altering the public perception of Christmas into something which emphasised family, religion, charity, social reconciliation and gift-giving rather than, er, just getting hammered.

Not a year goes by without some tabloid headline about Christmas being rebranded as 'Winterval' or people saying 'Happy Holidays' so as not to offend non-Christians.

Dickens's *A Christmas Carol*, which was published in 1843 and became instantly popular, was particularly instrumental in this regard – not least for bringing the phrase 'Merry Christmas' into public discourse.[23] The same year saw the production of the first commercial Christmas card (*see* Chapter 5.) And Victoria's marriage to the German Prince Albert also helped: Christmas was at the time a much larger celebration in Germany than

---

23 An excellent question for bluffers to ask their friends: What does Scrooge do? What's his job? A moneylender, right? Wrong. The answer is that you never find out, at least not in Dickens's book. He's just described as a miser. Some film versions have him as a moneylender, though.

it was here, and Albert brought many of his nation's customs over with him.[24]

20TH-CENTURY EVOLUTION

The significance of Christmas was further enhanced by the 1914 ceasefire, exchanging of gifts and staging of football matches between German and British troops in No Man's Land during the First World War.[25] But progress was still slow, and it wasn't until after the Second World War that Christmas really became the preserve of anyone beyond the well-off. Christmas trees, turkeys, stockings filled with anything other than fruit or maybe sweets too: these were all relatively rare. It was only in 1961 that postal deliveries on Christmas Day were discontinued, and Christmas Day football matches still continued in Scotland until the 1970s.[26] Many pubs and clubs now open on Christmas Day, confirming that not everybody buys into the festive family spirit at home.

Even as well-established as it is today, Christmas is often portrayed as being under attack. Not a year goes by without some tabloid headline about Christmas

---

24 Those of you who know what a 'Prince Albert' is without googling, settle down at the back there. (For those who don't, it involves the trouser department.)

25 This was directly responsible for Paul McCartney's 'Pipes of Peace', however, thus proving that every silver lining has a cloud.

26 Nowadays, of course, the big Christmas day for football matches is Boxing Day, meaning that the 22 people on the pitch have eaten low-fat high-protein nutritional food the day before, and the 58,936 people in the stands need wheelbarrows to help transport their distended stomachs.

being rebranded as 'Winterval'[27] or people saying 'Happy Holidays' so as not to offend non-Christians. These headlines always come from the same papers which also without fail every year predict a barbecue summer (translation: mild and wet), the worst winter in living memory (translation: mild and wet) and the permanent demise of the Lib Dems (translation: mild and wet).

---

27 The worst rebranding since Ipswich tried to reinforce its credentials as a young, hip, tech-savvy place by calling itself either 'Hipswich' or 'I.P. Town.'

FATHER CHRISTMAS

> **ON the Third Day of Christmas, gifts received to date from True Love:**
>
> **three French hens,**
> **four turtle doves,**
> **and three partridges in a pear tree.**

An elderly man with a penchant for wearing red, a white beard and promising equitable distribution to all people. But that's enough about Jeremy Corbyn.

Like many of our Christmas traditions, Father Christmas has, *Dr Who*-style, gone through several different incarnations over the centuries before becoming how we know him today. As the personification of Christmas, Father Christmas first appeared during Oliver Cromwell's interregnum following the English Civil War midway through the 17th century. Cromwell's Puritans had outlawed Christmas, prompting royalist political pamphleteers to adopt 'Old Father Christmas' as a symbol of (better and more enjoyable) times past.[28] This character concerned himself chiefly with eating, drinking and having a good time.[29]

AMERICAN MAKEOVER

As with Christmas in general, Father Christmas only began to take on the characteristics we recognise during Victorian times. But where other changes had come from home-grown writers such as Dickens[30] or the German influence brought over by Prince Albert, Father Christmas's Victorian evolution was most heavily influenced from across the Atlantic.

For the Americans, the personification of Christmas was called Santa Claus, himself derived from the 4th century Greek bishop St Nicholas who was well known for his benevolence in giving gifts to the poor.

In 1822, the American writer and academic Clement Clarke Moore wrote ''Twas The Night Before Christmas'. Bluffer klaxon! ''Twas the night before Christmas' is the first line of the poem, but not its title, which is 'A Visit from St Nicholas'. Bonus bluffer points for knowing that Moore owned the Chelsea country estate just outside

---

28 Their message, in effect, was 'restore the monarchy and be merry'. Nowadays they'd have to go through endless focus groups and a client who kept changing their mind literally minutes before sign-off.

29 Definitely not Jeremy Corbyn, then.

30 Curiously, Father Christmas does appear, sort of, in *A Christmas Carol*: more specifically, in John Leech's illustration of the Ghost of Christmas Present, who wears a holly wreath and a loose, furred gown (albeit in green rather than red).

New York (and made a mint when it was developed as part of the city's expansion) and also compiled a vast dictionary of ancient Hebrew. He wrote 'A Visit From St. Nicholas' for his children, never expecting it to go beyond the family, let alone become globally famous; but every Christmas Eve millions of parents read it to millions of children. The ancient Hebrew dictionary, less so.

Historically, Clement Clarke Moore has been credited with the poem, but many scholars now believe the occasional poet and New York grandee Major Henry Livingston Jr to have been the author. Bluffers don't have to take sides, but should nonetheless be aware of the controversy. [31]

Livingston/Moore's poem contains many of Christmas's modern-day tropes:

- Santa's sleigh is pulled by eight reindeer, though Rudolf and his red nose are not among them (these ones are called Dasher, Dancer, Prancer, Vixen, Comet, Cupid, Donner und Blitzen). The latter two, translated as 'Thunder and Lightning' earned worldwide recognition as a popular exclamation denoting surprise and disbelief.
- Santa himself has 'a broad face and a little round belly/That shook when he laughed, like a bowl full of jelly'.
- He comes equipped with presents: 'A bundle of

---

[31] It's a little like the whole Shakespeare/Earl of Oxford thing, but with more reindeer and fewer witches/star-crossed lovers/choice of which pencil to use (2B or not 2B).

toys he had flung on his back, And he looked like a
peddler just opening his pack.'
* And he enters and leaves through the chimney,
though this harks back many centuries: pre-
Christian Norse tradition had the god Odin making
his solstice visits into houses through chimneys
and fire-holes, and many cultures hold the hearth
sacred as a source of beneficence.

Despite the reindeer and sleigh, Moore did not, however,
specify exactly where Santa lived. The choice of 90.0000 N
0.0000 W[32] (or, as it's more commonly known, the North
Pole) was probably that of cartoonist Thomas Nast, who
drew several images for *Harper's* and other publications in
the 1860s alluding to Santa and the North Pole. Canadian
children who write to Santa will indeed find him at
the North Pole (for these purposes under Canadian
jurisdiction) with the postal code H0H 0H0.

THE SANTA SYMBIOSIS

The two figures, Father Christmas and Santa Claus, might
have started out as very different entities, but they soon
became more or less synonymous with each other: by the
turn of the century their names were being used pretty
much interchangeably, and in 1915 *Punch* magazine said
that 'the majority of children today do not know of any
difference between our old Father Christmas and the

---

32 In fact, any and all longitudes fit: the North Pole, like the South Pole,
has all possible longitudes at the same time. This is your free copy of *The
Bluffer's Guide To Polar Co-ordinates*.

comparatively new Santa Claus, as, by both wearing the same garb, they have effected a happy compromise'.

It's commonly assumed that the red outfit was only finally settled on following a 1931 Coca-Cola advertising campaign, but in fact White Rock Beverages had already used a similar image in two previous campaigns (for mineral water in 1915 and ginger ale in 1923), and *Puck* magazine had featured a red-and-white Santa on several of its covers early in the 20th century.

SUPER SANTA

Few aspects of modern life are immune from technology, and Santa is no exception. In 1955, a Sears Roebuck store in Colorado Springs gave out the number of a 'Santa hotline' which children could call. But the number was mistyped, and the one printed was that of the Continental Air Defense Command (CONAD). CONAD's Director of Operations, Colonel Harry Shoup, answered the calls by telling children that Santa was being tracked on radar, and so began the tradition of what is now NORAD Tracks Santa (NORAD being the North American Air Defense Command, jointly founded by the USA and Canada in 1958). Every Christmas Eve, the NORAD website follows a computer-generated sleigh across the world, together with a running total of the number of presents Santa's delivered.

All of which, of course, begs the question: How does he do it? The following assumptions can safely be made:

- that Santa has an enormous warehousing and distribution facility, with state-of-the-art computerised management systems and highly trained elves on excellent incentive programmes

- that Santa can deliver to all 1.9bn children in the world, whether or not they believe in him, because he's nice like that
- that, even though he clearly has the kind of total surveillance capacities any government would kill for (he not only knows where every child lives, but can also judge their annual standards of behaviour according to the naughty/nice dynamic), he still chooses to use those capacities benevolently and not withhold presents from any child, no matter how much of a brat they might be (yes, Tyler from number 32 across the road, you know who you are)
- that these children are distributed evenly across households, which are themselves distributed evenly across the world (neither is strictly true, but for the purposes of mathematical modelling they're as good a framework as any)
- that Santa's smart enough to use the rotation of the earth in his favour, starting on the International Date Line and working his way east to west across the time zones, thus giving him 32 hours of Christmas Eve rather than 24.

Given all these assumptions, Santa, his reindeer and sleigh would have to be moving at an average speed of more than 5 million mph,[33]:and that's not even taking account of:

---

33 No wonder Rudolf's nose is red.

- the need to dodge certain areas (military bases, restricted airspace around major airports, war zones, rogue states, drones . . .)
- the sleigh's payload (those presents are heavy, you know)
- the friction caused by air resistance on such a large object[34]
- the constant accelerations and decelerations involved in entering and leaving 5,000 houses per second, which would subject Santa and the reindeer to G-forces way in excess of what any living being could survive.[35]

The antlers are actually fractal vortex-shedding devices. We are talking not aerodynamics here, but antlaerodynamics.

The only possible solution, therefore, is that Santa has discovered some sort of quantum physics allowing him to travel substantially in excess of the speed of light, meaning that our 32 hours equate to up to 364

---

34 Let's be honest, Santa himself could do with slimming down a bit too, though maybe when you have several million presents on the same sleigh as you, a couple of extra stones aren't going to make that much difference.

35 Ensuring that the reindeer have sufficient calories is the easy bit: all those mince pies which people leave out are chock full of sugar, which will keep the reindeer going all night, even if they do have teeth like Elizabeth I by the end.

days in his own timeframe. Professor Ian Stewart, Warwick University maths professor, has theorised that the reindeer may be the key to all this. 'Reindeer have a curious arrangement of gadgetry on top of their heads which we call antlers and naively assume exist for the males to do battle and to win females. This is absolute nonsense. The antlers are actually fractal vortex-shedding devices. We are talking not aerodynamics here, but antlaerodynamics.'[36]

Then again, if Santa has access to such advanced science he's almost certainly learned how to clone himself too, so perhaps there's not just one Santa but thousands, each responsible for their own small corner of the world ('What do you mean, Schleswig-Holstein's mine? That's Andreas's responsibility. It's *always* been Andreas's responsibility.')

---

36 The faster the reindeer go, the less likely it is that Rudolph's nose will in fact remain red. According to the Doppler shift, which astronomers use to assess how fast stars and galaxies are moving in relation to us, a stationary observer will see an object turn, in sequence, yellow, green, blue, violet, and finally invisible (ultraviolet) as its speed increases.

ALL DECKED OUT

Just as the Roman festival of Saturnalia was the precursor to Christmas, so too were the fir trees which the Romans used to decorate their temples during the festival, the precursor to modern-day Christmas trees. It wasn't just the Romans who used trees during the winter months: many European peoples put up evergreens, or planted bushes, or made pyramids of fruit and vegetables, all as a reminder that spring and summer would return, that

33

the natural cycle would go on, and that plants would grow again.[37]

Fast forward the best part of a millennium and a half, and it was the Germans who made most of the running in popularising the concept of the Christmas tree. Martin Luther is popularly supposed to have been the first person to bring a tree indoors after walking through a forest, seeing how beautiful the pines looked with stars twinkling through the branches, and trying to recreate the effect with candles. Nowadays, of course, he'd have Extinction Rebellion denouncing him as an environmental terrorist.[38]

---

[37] A similar reasoning is behind the prevalence of mistletoe at Christmas: its evergreen nature made it ideal for display round about the winter solstice. Mistletoe also plays a central role in Norse mythology: the god Baldr had a dream of his own death, and so his mother Frigg made every object on earth vow not to harm him. However, she forgot mistletoe, and so the trickster god Loki made a spear from the plant and got Baldr's brother Höðr to inadvertently kill Baldr with it. (So far, so bog standard family Christmas.) Mistletoe was also an ancient fertility symbol, which may partly explain why people are enjoined to kiss beneath it. It was certainly a tradition come Victorian times: in *The Pickwick Papers*, Charles Dickens described how young women 'screamed and struggled, and ran into corners, and did everything but leave the room, until they all at once found it useless to resist any longer and submitted to be kissed with a good grace'.

[38] Luther is perhaps best known for nailing his 95 *Theses* to the door of All Saints' Church in Wittenberg in 1517. Only after doing so did he think of five more which would have made a nice round number. He also stood firm against contemporary obsessions with witchcraft when recording his seminal track 'I Got 95 Theses (And a Witch Ain't One)'. In later years, his ghost was reported to have been 'really annoyed' that he hadn't thought of the 'I have a dream' line first.

> Christmas trees came to Britain from Germany in the way many customs crossed borders in those days: through intermarriage between various European branches of royalty.

GEMÜTLICHKEIT

The Germans liked the fact that Christmas trees were examples of *gemütlichkeit*, which is another excellent bluffer word meaning a sense of warmth, cosiness and good cheer. Christmas trees were also recorded in Livonia (modern-day Estonia and Latvia), where the Brotherhood of Blackheads would erect trees in their guild houses and the town squares of Reval (now Tallinn) and Riga.[39]

Christmas trees came to Britain from Germany in the way many customs crossed borders in those days: through intermarriage between various European branches of royalty. Charlotte of Mecklenburg-Strelitz, George III's wife, introduced a Christmas tree to a children's party in 1800.

---

39 A little disappointingly, perhaps, the Brotherhood of Blackheads is nothing to do with clogged hair follicles and blocked skin pores, and do not therefore hold their meetings in the nearest branch of Boots (third Tuesday of every month, by the skincare aisle, don't be late). But since they provided Reval with, among other things, a cavalry detachment, 8 rock-hurling machines, 20 cannon carriages and 66 small-calibre guns, we can surmise that (a) they were pretty kickass and (b) their version of 'The Twelve Days of Christmas' never really caught on.

As a child, the then Princess Victoria had a tree in her bedroom every Christmas, and her journal for Christmas Eve 1832, when she was 13, records that 'after dinner we went into the drawing-room near the dining-room. There were two large round tables on which were placed two trees hung with lights and sugar ornaments. All the presents being placed round the trees…'

The first recorded instance of Prince Albert setting up a tree at Windsor Castle was in 1841; seven years later, the practice became widespread (at least among the well-to-do) after the royal family and their tree were featured on the cover of *The Illustrated London News*. Trees became a common part of all Christmas celebrations by the mid-1920s, and today almost 8 million real trees are sold in Britain every year. In the US the figure is closer to 30 million.

There are also the trees donated by other nations in the spirit of friendship and gratitude. Most people know that every year Norway presents London with a tree (a Norway spruce, naturally) which stands in Trafalgar Square as thanks for the city's support during the Second World War (King Haakon formed a government-in-exile in London and became a symbol of Norwegian resistance against the Nazis), but only the hardcore bluffer will know that several other British cities receive trees from other Norwegian cities or regions. Aberdeen and Sunderland receive one each from Stavanger, Edinburgh and the Orkneys one each from Hordaland, Grimsby one from Sortland, and Newcastle one from Bergen. If asked, bluffers won't be far from the truth by venturing that the reasons for these annual gifts range from recognition of wartime solidarity to celebration of a shared Viking heritage (however tenuous).

A Christmas tree is, of course, not simply a Christmas tree. When it comes to what, where, when and how, the bluffer will be able to guide the less enlightened through thickets[40] of confusion.

What?

You basically have four choices: fir, spruce, pine or artificial. The Nordmann fir is expensive but looks great and retains its needles well. The Fraser fir is narrower, which can work well when space is limited. The Norway spruce has a lovely rich green colour and a delicious fragrance. The blue spruce holds its needles better but can be pricklier. The Scots pine has strong branches which can support heavy decorations, and is the only genuinely native pine in the UK.

Artificial trees are in general cheaper and, obviously, last longer. Whether or not they're your bag depends on how wedded you are to a traditional tree, and how concerned you are about environmental issues: various studies have shown that artificial trees have to be used for up to 20 years before their carbon footprint is as small as that of an organic tree.

Where?

The most obvious point about the optimum location for a Christmas tree is also one of the most ignored: make sure there's enough room! It's not just height that's the

---

40 Pun intended, obviously, like all groanworthy ones are.

issue (and remember that the tree will be even taller once you've put a star/angel/Teenage Mutant Ninja Turtle on top) but width too: trees become wider in the first couple of hours after setting up as their branches settle.

In addition, make sure there's room for people to put down and pick up presents under the tree, that the tree's not too near a radiator (which will dry it out) and that pets and young children can't cause havoc anywhere near enough to risk bringing the tree down.

When?

Traditionally, Christmas trees were not put up until Christmas Eve and were taken down by 6 January, the day after Twelfth Night.

The former is no longer true. When you choose to put your Christmas tree up depends on several things – whether you have children, where you live, the state of your hangover following the company works do – but in any case it should never be earlier than 1 December. Jumping the gun before then just looks too keen, and no self-respecting bluffer wants that.

The latter is still true, not just because to leave it up longer is considered bad luck but also because by this stage trees will be shedding their needles quicker than middle-aged men are losing their hair (most cut trees last between four and six weeks).

How?

Before buying, check a tree's freshness by (a) seeing whether there are lots of needles on the ground beneath it and (b) placing your hand on a branch where it meets the trunk and pulling gently towards you, again to see whether needles fall off.

Saw about an inch off the bottom of the trunk before setting the tree in its base. This will help the tree absorb as much water as it needs, and it will, perhaps up to a gallon a day. Many people (but not bluffers) will be surprised to learn that a real tree needs to be kept hydrated. Keep the stand topped up with water, and never let the water level go below the tree's base. Make sure your stand fits your tree, and that you don't have to whittle down the sides of the trunk: the outer layers of wood are most efficient in taking up water.

Wait an hour or two after putting the tree up before starting to decorate it: this gives the branches time to settle. Start your decorating with the lights, beginning at the top and working your way down. Nestle wires in the branches to hide them. If you think you have too many lights, you probably have just about enough. Plug them in and turn them on before you move on to the next phase: if they're not working, or they're not in the right places, now's the time you need to find out.

Then put ribbons and tinsel on, and after them the baubles and other decorations. Hang larger and heavier baubles nearer the trunk, and smaller, lighter ones nearer the ends of the branches. Finish off with the topper, and then pour yourself a drink. It's Christmas, after all.

Candles? Caution! They look lovely but in terms of fire risk they're an accident waiting to happen. Bluffer's Health and Safety – sorry, sorry, Elf 'n Safety – counsels that, if you do want to go down the candle route, make sure they're securely fastened to a stable surface, that there's nothing flammable within reach, and that they can't be tipped over by children, dogs or wind (as in breeze from outside as opposed to the inevitable result of excess Brussels sprout consumption).

When it comes to taking the tree down, obviously do all this in reverse. If you have a garden, consider using your old tree as a bird feeder rather than just sending it to be recycled. Stringing bird food from the tree's branches will bring all kinds of local birds to it. If you have a pond, sinking the tree into it provides a lovely habitat for fish and tadpoles, and saves claiming for a duck house on your parliamentary expenses.

CHRISTMAS COMMS

ON the Fifth Day of Christmas, gifts received to date from True Love:

five gold rings,
eight calling birds,
nine French hens,
eight turtle doves,
five partridges in a pear tree. . . .

When does Advent begin? 1 December, right?

Wrong.

Well, wrong six years out of seven. (Don't choose that seventh year to make this point to your non-bluffer friends, obviously.) Advent actually begins on the Sunday nearest to 30 November, St Andrew's Day.[41]

---

41 St Andrew himself provides rich pickings for the bluffer. Bronze-level bluffing: he's the patron saint of Scotland. Silver-level bluffing: he was one of Jesus's 12 apostles. Gold-level bluffing: he was crucified by the Romans upside down on a saltire (an X-shaped cross, as seen on the Scottish flag) because according to tradition he felt unworthy to die in the same way as Jesus Christ.

But in 1908, Gerhard Lang of Swabia in south-west Germany, remembering how his mother had sewn cookies on to the lid of a box and allowed him to eat one a day during Advent, started to manufacture Advent calendars commercially. To save the time and costs involved in altering the start date every year, he simply fixed it as 1 December, meaning that every calendar could be made according to the same 24-window template.[42]

The 1 December start date has bled through into many aspects of Christmas. Not only is it seen as *infra dig* to put up your tree before then, but also to send Christmas cards before then.

By now, of course, it should be clear to the bluffer that pretty much everything about modern Christmas comes from (a) the Victorians, (b) the Germans or (c) both. Christmas cards are no exception, being fully Victorian (though not at all German) in concept. In 1843, Henry Cole (who also founded the Victoria and Albert Museum) found himself deluged with letters from friends, acquaintances and colleagues.

Since he was too busy to reply to each one individually, he commissioned John Callcott Horsley to print him 1,000 3.75-inch by 5-inch lithograph cards illustrated with scenes of three generations of a family raising a toast to the card's recipient, and of food and

---

42 The well-known meme of a Scottish Advent calendar being simply a 24-can pack of Tennant's Extra is scurrilous, blasphemous, insulting, and extremely funny.

clothing being given to the poor. All Cole had to do was sign his name in each one.[43]

It should be clear to the bluffer that pretty much everything about modern Christmas comes from
(a) the Victorians, (b) the Germans or (c) both.

Despite the inexpensive cost of posting cards – the Uniform Penny Post had been introduced three years previously – the cards themselves were still relatively pricey at a shilling each,[44] and the image of children drinking wine perhaps understandably proved a touch controversial to Victorian mores, so it was a few years before the habit really caught on.

Now, of course, every postman with seasonal afflictive lumbago curses Cole heartily for the entire duration of December. Electronic alternatives have made traditional Christmas cards less popular than they had previously been, but they're still sold, sent and delivered in vast numbers: more than 1bn Christmas cards were bought

---

43 Demonstrating a commendable grasp of Christmas's commercial opportunities, Cole sold off the cards he didn't use.

44 If you can find one today, it'll cost you a lot more than a shilling. A card from Cole's first batch was sold at auction in 2001 for £22,250, the most expensive Christmas card in history.

in the UK in 2017 alone, accounting for 45% of the entire annual greetings card market.[45]

A 2018 Royal Mail study of more than 2,000 people showed that 77% of people still give Christmas cards by way of spreading festive cheer, ahead of well-wishes in person (62%), text (34%), Facebook message (26%), WhatsApp (21%) and pouring alcohol down their throat (question not asked, sadly). More than 50% said they liked displaying the cards in their home, with 45% enjoying the thrill of receiving something through the post.[46]

Mark Street, Royal Mail's head of campaigns, said, 'There's something inherently festive and heartwarming about sending and receiving a physical card through the post, which someone has lovingly taken the time to write. Put simply, sometimes a letter or card is better.' (Not to mention pretty essential to you still having a job to come to on Monday morning, Mark, but anyway.)

Cards come from far and wide. The bluffer, being a well-travelled type of cove, will be able to say 'Merry Christmas and Happy New Year' not just in English but at least two dozen European languages, including some obscure ones which will hint at long-term deep-cover cultural immersion:

---

45 Only 15% of Christmas cards are bought by men. That sound you can hear is every single woman reading this bit gasping in disbelief and wondering exactly which men comprise this 15% – since she sure as hell doesn't know any of them.

46 By 'something through the post', they presumably meant something that wasn't a tax demand, a utility company's final reminder, a pizza flyer or the local newsletter featuring articles on parish history which can bring on gravity-warping ennui to all those brave enough to read them.

- **Albanian**: Gëzuar Krishtlindjet dhe Vitin e Ri
- **Croatian**: Hrvatski: Čestit Božić i sretna Nova godina
- **Czech**: Veselé vánoce a šťastný nový rok
- **Danish**: Glædelig jul og godt nytår!
- **Dutch**: Prettige kerstdagen en een gelukkig nieuwjaar
- **Estonian**: Häid jõule ja head uut aastat
- **Finnish**: Hyvää joulua ja onnellista uutta vuotta
- **French**: Joyeux Noël et Bonne Année
- **German**: Fröhliche Weihnachten und ein gutes Neues Jahr
- **Hungarian**: Kellemes karácsonyi ünnepeket és boldog új évet
- **Icelandic**: Gleðileg jól og farsælt nýtt ár
- **Irish**: Nollaig Shona Duit
- **Italian**: Buon Natale e Felice Anno Nuovo
- **Latvian**: Priecīgus Ziemassvētkus un laimīgu Jauno gadu
- **Lithuanian**: Linksmų šventų Kalėdų ir laimingų Naujųjų metų
- **Norwegian**: God jul og godt nyttår
- **Polish**: Wesołych Świąt i Szczęśliwego Nowego Roku
- **Portuguese**: Feliz Natal e um Feliz Ano Novo
- **Romanian**: Crăciun Fericit şi La mulţi ani
- **Slovak**: Veselé Vianoce a Štastný Nový rok
- **Slovenian**: Vesel Božič in Srečno Novo Leto
- **Spanish**: Feliz Navidad y próspero Año Nuevo
- **Swedish**: God Jul och Gott Nytt År
- **Welsh**: Nadolig Llawen a Blwyddyn Newydd Dda

There are three main types of round-robin letter, which themselves can be easily remembered with the BBC mnemonic: the Boastful, the Boring and the Catastrophic.

Christmas cards are all well and good, obviously, but if you want to go to next-level festive communication you really need the round-robin letter. A family you don't see from one year to the next (not least because they do this kind of thing) send several pages of A4 recapping their year. The bluffer knows that there are three main types of round-robin letter, which themselves can be easily remembered with the BBC mnemonic: the Boastful, the Boring and the Catastrophic.

I. **The Boastful**. Details the sender's myriad accomplishments in a tone of pitch-perfect humble-bragging. Get one of these, and you've been smugged. You know how it goes: something like this.

'Wow! We can hardly believe where the last 12 months have gone! So much has happened, and we've hardly been at home – Courchevel, Antigua, Dubai, Umbria and South Africa, and that was just the first half of the year. John was lucky enough to make partner this year, which means he's working even harder than before (hard to believe that's possible!) but of course the pay rise is some compensation. Jane has been project managing the renovation of our holiday home in Dordogne (there goes the money from John's pay rise, and probably more besides!), Archie got A* or A in all 44 of his GCSEs, and Bella is in the county hockey team (she would have been captain but the coach said she was so good that it would be unfair on all the other children).'

Of course, these letters are usually works of fiction, not so much in what they say as what they don't say. Here are ten of the most common euphemisms which the bluffer will easily be able to decode:

What they say	What they mean
James is always away on business	James is having an affair
Susie is enjoying her tennis lessons	Susie is having an affair too
We had an amazing silver wedding party	You weren't invited
And are looking forward to another one in 25 years' time	You won't be invited to that one either
Hannah has taken to motherhood like a duck to water	A more appropriate aquatic simile would be 'Hannah is drinking like a fish'
We had an amazing holiday. So nice to spend time with each other	We'll be paying off the credit card till 2040 and we sat in resentful silence most evenings

What they say	What they mean
Matilda has a seriously fun group of friends	If one or more of them doesn't get locked up I'll eat my hat
Our garden is looking lovely	Our garden is looking better than next door's
Hope you and yours are well	We have no idea what your family's names are
We must, must, MUST catch up this year	We will never see each other again

II. **The Boring**. These go into the kind of minute detail usually reserved for scientists examining objects through electron microscopes.

'In July we went to France. The flight was delayed several hours, but luckily we had enough water to keep well hydrated. On arrival at Toulouse airport, we found that the car hire company had messed up our reservation, meaning we had to make do with an Opel estate with 12,000km on the clock rather than the new BMW X3 with head-up display which Gavin had specifically requested. Bad went to worse when roadworks on the autoroute added further time to our journey and ensured that, despite the Opel's exceptionally efficient climate control system, tempers were beginning to boil over. ...' (Continues in similar vein for 640 further pages.)

III. **The Catastrophic.** Family illnesses, pet deaths, gruesome operations, embarrassing medical conditions, redundancies, divorce, debt and pretty much every other conceivable form of bad news, all recounted with a relish which is hidden beneath the deadpan delivery but still definitely there. Imagine watching every movie Ingmar Bergman ever made while listening to Joy Division on a sodden November afternoon, and you'll be about a tenth of the way to how singularly depressing this kind of round-robin letter is.

'Well, what a year it's been. Keith was admitted to hospital for what we thought would be a routine gallbladder operation but instead ended up as a three-month stay battling MRSA superbugs and NHS cutbacks ("Ooh, little bit of politics", as Ben Elton used to say.) By the time he was out he found he was also suffering from what we can coyly describe as "middle-aged man problems" (you know, the ones which the blue pills are for). Meanwhile, Sarah's business went into administration. ...'

How the bluffer chooses to deal with a round-robin letter depends on the category into which it falls:

- To the boastful, reply asking why the son-in-law, whose achievements were so lauded in years 2009–18 inclusive, has now been airbrushed from history in a frankly Stalinist manner following the divorce.
- To the boring, mark it as though it were an essay, highlighting factual inconsistencies and poor grammar, and send it back to them.
- To the catastrophic, send one yourself with a (hopefully) fictional account of your own *annus horribilis*, written in the requisite absurdly jocular tone. 'Christopher is earning excellent money

selling crack to kids in the local park, though he has decided to take a five-year sabbatical in the Wormwood Scrubs area of west London. Sally made history by being the first person ever to get a negative score in Maths GCSE. She really is a girl in a million!'

HERE WE COME A-CAROLLING

Of all the things Christmas is not Christmas without, Christmas is not Christmas without carols. (Try saying that after a few eggnogs.)

The first recorded instance of Christmas carols in England[47] came in 1426, when Shropshire chaplain John

---

47 'Recorded' as in 'written down', obviously, not 'recorded' as in 'making a permanent digital record of soundwaves arranged in a particular way'. Apple's takeover of the world may be well under way, but even they haven't yet invented a time machine to pop an iPod back into the Middle Ages.

Awdlay listed 25 'caroles of Cristemas'. These would almost certainly have been sung by wassailers[48] going in groups from house to house rather than in church, and the 'caroles' would have been general communal songs used during all kinds of celebrations rather than specifically Christmas tunes. The word 'carol' comes from the Old French *carole*, a circle dance accompanied by singers (which was in turn derived from the Latin *choraula*). The medieval chord patterns of such songs persist to this day in the carols we know and love, which is why they sound so distinctive.

Church carols were probably introduced after the Reformation – the Lutherans were pretty keen on music – though for a long time they would have been sung in Latin (hence 'O Come All Ye Faithful's' original title of 'Adeste Fideles', which is still used in places). As with so many aspects of Christmas, they really became popular in the 19th century: William Sandys' 1833 *Christmas Carols Ancient and Modern* included, for the first time in print, carols such as 'God Rest Ye Merry, Gentlemen; The First Noel'; and 'Hark! The Herald Angels Sing'.

The Christmas carol service itself dates from 1880, when Edward White Benson, Bishop of Truro, decided to hold such a service on Christmas Eve in an attempt to stop the townspeople getting hog-whimperingly drunk, as they had done on every

---

48 If the word 'wassailer' sounds like a euphemism for 'pisshead', that's not too far from the truth. The term could mean either a singer or a reveller, and the two were not exactly mutually exclusive. Safe to say that 15th-century carol singing was not so much beautiful schoolboy descant as a bawdy rugby club singalong kind of thing.

Christmas Eve from 1879 back through the mists of time.[49]

'I owe my entire career to my experience as a chorister . . . it was where I learnt the wonderful truth that something exceptional, something as beautiful as anything anywhere, can be created just by you and your friends.'

Alexander Armstrong

Nowadays, of course, Christmas carol services are ten a penny. But the daddy of them all is the Service of Nine Lessons and Carols from King's College, Cambridge, which begins just after 3 o'clock on Christmas Eve, which is listened to around the world, and which for many people marks the real start of Christmas proper. The choristers all attend King's College School, and the bluffer should know two things about this service and another thing about schoolboy choristers in general:

1.   The boy who is chosen to sing the solo which begins the service – the first verse of 'Once in Royal David's

---

49 The Benson family were quite something. Edward himself later became Archbishop of Canterbury, his wife had 39 lesbian lovers (all recorded in her diary), and among his sons were the novelist E.F. Benson and the poet Arthur Benson, both of them gay at a time when homosexuality was still very much illegal. Arthur wrote the words to 'Land of Hope and Glory'.

City' – only finds out that he's been chosen literally a few seconds beforehand. This is to stop him getting too nervous beforehand. The choirmaster watches a system of red lights during the 3pm Radio 4 news, and when the lights start flashing that means there are ten seconds left and the announcer's saying that they're crossing live to King's College Chapel. It's at this point that the choirmaster points to one of the boys (there are usually around 16, and the chosen one will almost always be in Year 8, his last year at the school, and maybe only weeks or months away from his voice breaking). This system has been used more or less constantly since the first broadcast in 1928.

2. There is a TV broadcast a couple of hours after the radio broadcast, but they aren't of the same service. The TV broadcast is recorded a few weeks beforehand to allow time for editing, and the format of the service may be slightly different. Sometimes, though not often, there are different soloists for the first verse of 'Once in Royal David's City'.

3. Schoolboy choristers go on to make their mark in many different walks of life, not just music. TV quiz master and comedian Alexander Armstrong was at St Mary's Cathedral, Edinburgh, actor Simon Russell Beale at St Paul's, wine expert Oz Clarke at Canterbury, cricketer Alistair Cook at Westminster Abbey, MP David Lammy at Peterborough, and newsreader Jon Snow at Winchester. Cook has attributed his discipline, patience and unflappability to his choir training. Armstrong has said 'I owe my entire career to my experience as a chorister. It was

where I learnt to perform, where I learnt to use the full range of my voice; where I learnt to listen, where I learnt to write comedy, where I learnt to carry a pencil at all times – but most importantly it was where I learnt the wonderful truth that something exceptional, something as beautiful as anything anywhere, can be created just by you and your friends.'

The bluffer will also be able to point the less erudite members of society in the direction of interesting facts about some of the best-known carols. As ever with bluffing, use this knowledge sparingly. A couple of well-dropped morsels will hint at measureless depths of knowledge; a running commentary for the duration of Nine Lessons and Carols will end up with things being thrown at you.

Anyway. Here in the spirit of Nine Lessons and Carols are, er, nine of the most popular carols with a little lesson about each of them – plus one wild card entry at the end.

- **Good King Wenceslas.** Based on a real person – Vaclav, 10th-century Duke of Bohemia – who wasn't a king and wasn't called Wenceslas. Vaclav's father died when he was young, leaving him to be brought up by his pagan mother and her Christian mother-in-law. You can see where this is going, can't you? It always comes back to some *Eastenders*-style Christmas eruption. Pagan mother had Christian mother-in-law strangled with a veil; Vaclav had pagan mother exiled when he came of age. He seems to have been a good egg: a contemporary account has him 'rising every night from his noble bed, with bare feet and only one chamberlain, he went around to God's churches and gave alms generously to widows, orphans, those in prison and afflicted by every difficulty, so much so that he was considered, not a prince, but the "father of all the wretched." In turn, Vaclav became a martyr after being killed by his bastard brother Boleslaw the Bad (a useful name to remember if you like alliteration).[50] Vaclav should have – you know this is coming – he should really have looked out, shouldn't he?[51]

- ***Hark! The Herald Angels Sing.*** Lyrics by Charles Wesley (one of more than 6,000 hymns credited to him), music by Felix Mendelssohn, who died without ever knowing that his tune had become a hymn. He originally wrote it about Johannes Gutenberg, inventor of the printing press,[52] and said he was happy to have it repurposed for any cause other than a religious one. Bit of a shame it fit Wesley's lyrics so perfectly, then. A very 18th/19th-century version of Elton John and Bernie Taupin. Sort of.

- ***In the Bleak Midwinter.*** Based on a poem by Christina Rossetti, it can be set to one of two different arrangements: Gustav Holst (1906) or Harold Darke (1911).

---

50 Nowadays Boleslaw with the Unresolved Anger Management Issues.

51 See also one of the oldest jokes in the world: How does King Wenceslas like his pizzas? Deep pan, crisp and even.

52 Something of a niche market, songs about typesetters, you'd have to say.

- *It Came upon the Midnight Clear.* Perhaps the carol most explicitly associated with war and peace:

  Yet with the woes of sin and strife
  The world has suffered long;
  Beneath the angel strain have rolled
  Two thousand years of wrong;
  And man, at war with man, hears not
  The love song which they bring;
  O hush the noise, ye men of strife,
  And hear the angels sing!

Written in 1849 by Massachusetts pastor Edmund Sears in the wake of the US's war with Mexico and revolutions in Europe. The music was written 25 years later by Arthur Sullivan – yes, as in 'Gilbert and …'.

- *O Come, O Come Emmanuel.* Translated from Latin to English in 1861, and composed in such a way that English and Latin words can be used interchangeably.
- *O Little Town of Bethlehem.* Written in 1868 by Rector Phillips Brooks, who was inspired by the view of Bethlehem from the Palestinian hills during a pilgrimage to the Holy Land. His church organist Lewis Redner wrote the melody for the local Sunday school choir three years later.
- *Once in Royal David's City.* Written in 1848 by children's poet Cecil Frances Alexander, who's also remembered for her hymn 'All Things Bright and Beautiful'. The carol was set to music a year later by organist H.J. Gauntlett.

- *Silent Night.* Originally the German 'Stille Nacht', composed in 1818 and translated into English in 1859. Sung by English and German troops alike during the Christmas truce of 1914.
- *The First Nowell.* Not originally French, as you might think from the similarity to 'Noël', but Cornish ('Nowell' is an old Anglo-Saxon spelling). Not to be confused with Exeter Chiefs and England rugby player Jack Nowell (even though he is originally Cornish himself).
- *The Twelve Days of Christmas.* Thought to be originally either French and/or designed as a memory game (*see* Glossary). The earliest known version appeared in the 1780 children's book *Mirth Without Mischief* (price of a first edition at auction: £18,800. Price of a paperback copy on a well-known tax-minimising online retail site which may or may not share its name with the largest river in South America: £13.99). The standard tune (including everyone's favourite bit, 'fiiiiive gooooold rinnnnngs') was arranged by Frederic Austin in 1909.

  The lyrics have changed in places over the years. 'Bears a-baiting' and 'ships a-sailing' have been mentioned in the past (presumably now discontinued on the grounds of animal cruelty and maritime safety respectively), as have 'colly birds' (birds as black as coal – i.e. blackbirds) rather than 'calling birds'.

  There is, however, little credence to the idea that the song contains coded references to Christianity in order to help persecuted Christians learn the mainstays of their faith in secret. (This is ideal bluffer's territory, of course, as the only thing better than propagating an obscure theory is dismantling it.) This theory holds that:

1. The partridge in a pear tree represents Jesus Christ
2. The two turtle doves represent the Old and New Testaments
3. The three French hens represent faith, hope and charity, the theological virtues
4. The four calling birds represent Matthew, Mark, Luke and John and/or their Gospels
5. The five gold rings represent the Pentateuch – the first five books of the Old Testament (Genesis, Exodus, Leviticus, Numbers and Deuteronomy)
6. The six geese a-laying represent the six days of creation
7. The seven swans a-swimming represent the seven sacraments of the Catholic Church (baptism, confirmation, the Eucharist, reconciliation, anointing of the sick, holy orders and matrimony)
8. The eight maids a-milking represent the eight beatitudes (blessings recounted by Jesus in his Sermon on the Mount)
9. The nine ladies dancing represent the nine fruits of the Holy Spirit (love, joy, peace, patience, kindness, goodness, faithfulness, gentleness, and self-control)
10. The ten lords a-leaping represent the Ten Commandments
11. The 11 pipers piping represent the 11 faithful apostles (i.e. all of them apart from Judas)
12. The 12 drummers drumming represent the 12 articles of the Apostle's Creed.

The bluffer can refute this theory by pointing out any or all the following: that there's no correlation between the song's gifts and what they're supposed to represent, thus making its use as an aide-memoire dubious to say the least; that Christians weren't especially persecuted at the time the song was thought to have been written (and if they had been, they certainly wouldn't have been able to celebrate Christmas and sing carols!); and that the tune's upbeat nature would hardly have been condoned by what was at the time a very serious Church.

CHRISTMAS PRESENTS

ON the Seventh Day of Christmas, gifts received to date from True Love:

7 swans a-swimming,
12 geese a-laying,
10 gold rings,
16 calling birds,
15 French hens,
12 turtle doves,
7 partridges in a pear tree.

GIVE AND TAKE

The giving and receiving of presents are among the things most closely associated with Christmas.[53] The

---

53 Particularly if you're under the age of ten (in which case the 'receiving' bit is more important than the 'giving' bit, but less important than the 'ripping all your presents open by 5.30am on Christmas Day and then bursting into sugar-rush induced tears that there's nothing else to look forward to till next Christmas).

tradition probably comes from the three Magi and their gifts of gold, frankincense and myrrh,[54] though exchanging gifts may also have been part of Saturnalia, and the legend of St Nicholas also fed into the narrative that Christmas is a time for presents.

That said, Christmas Eve and/or Christmas Day are only relatively recent choices as prime present days. Bluffers should know that before the 19th century, the most popular dates for gift-giving were either St Nicholas's saint's day on 6 December, or around the New Year. The publications of 'A Visit from St Nicholas' and 'A Christmas Carol' in 1823 and 1843 respectively helped guide a gradual shift towards the dates we now accept as usual, and by the end of the 19 century the majority of presents were being exchanged around 24 and 25 December.

The bluffer will also point out the psychological as well as historical reasons behind giving presents. Leaving aside relentless consumerist pressure as part of late-era capitalist hegemony (that's enough out of you, Karl Marx – Ed.), gift-giving has long been a symbol in many cultures of investment in a relationship with another person, be that relationship romantic, family, friendship or business. This applies even beyond humans: for example, male penguins often present their preferred female with a pebble.[55]

---

54 Nowadays, of course, they'd have brought Red Dead Redemption 2, Harry Potter Lego and a BB-8 model droid. And there'd probably be couriers on zero-hour contracts who'd leave a card outside the stable door saying 'Sorry we missed you. We'll try to redeliver on the next working day.'

55 Try that this Christmas with your beloved and you can bet your life you'll be seeking a new beloved by Boxing Day.

It is a generalisation, though perhaps not too much of one, to suggest that, though the deadline for all Christmas present buying is by definition 24 December, the female of the species approaches the process in a considerably different manner from the male of the species.

THE FEMALE GIVER

Take a married couple with children. The wife must buy presents for: her husband; their children; her parents; his parents; her siblings, nieces, nephews, cousins and godchildren; his siblings, nieces, nephews, cousins and godchildren; and of course herself, as he will almost certainly forget/get it wrong/give her the same present as last year (or all three, consecutively).

The husband must buy presents for: his wife. (*See* previous paragraph.)

The wife will, no later than the summer solstice on 21 June (thus giving her six months), draw up a spreadsheet, listing: all necessary recipients; maximum spend per person; suitable presents based on interests/ age; and all of the above cross-referenced to previous years to avoid duplication of presents. She will become especially exercised by what to buy her husband, not just because he will already just have bought himself anything he likes the look of already, but also because if she gives him anything unexpected he will assume it to be a Trojan horse in her endless plans to give him a makeover and render him more suitable for public display. She will go online to price comparison and other retail websites, factoring in upcoming sales, currency movements, seasonal crazes and sundry additional relevant factors. Once the actual purchasing begins, she will adopt the kind of ruthless organisation which would shame the military, colour-coding purchases on receipt and stacking them neatly in an area of the house subject to password control and general lockdown. It is usually known as the 'safe room'. She will maintain this rigid delineation of presents by using different wrapping paper per distinct set of recipients. For those recipients who won't be seen over the festive period, she will post in good time to beat the Christmas rush. For those who will be seen but necessitate travelling, she will store their presents neatly in the car boot. For those who will be seen on Christmas Day itself, she will stack them neatly beneath the Christmas tree. And she will, of course, indignantly refute all accusations of being anally retentive.

THE MALE GIVER

The husband will, in contrast, maintain his usual schedule (five-a-side, curry, Friday nights in the pub) well into the autumn and early winter. He will become vaguely aware that Christmas is approaching, but mainly due to the increased frequency of parties which he feels obliged to go to[56]. He will wait till Christmas

---

56 They're work dos, mainly. Or perhaps client stuff. He doesn't really want to go to them. That's why he's always the last to leave at 2am, having got his company's main supplier in a drunken headlock and informed him that he's his best mate, he really is, and he loves him, he really loves him.

Eve. Not the morning of Christmas Eve, either. The afternoon. Late afternoon. He will panic. He will run to the shops, pausing halfway to get his breath back as all that partying has left him a little short of peak physical condition. He will look round frantically, his head swivelling like Linda Blair's in *The Exorcist*[57]. He will remember four precious words. 'Shit in a basket!' Not an injunction but a description. A selection of body wash, lotion, soap etc. In a basket. Women love that stuff, he will think. He will buy it. He will return home. And only while wrapping it, inexpertly, that night will he get a sense of déjà vu, and realise he bought exactly the same thing for her last Christmas, and very probably the Christmas before that too.

GENERAL SPECIFICS

Generalisations over, on to specifics. These are the things the bluffer should know:

How much to spend

One in three people use credit cards or overdrafts to partially or fully fund their seasonal spending. The average household spends around £500 on Christmas presents. Clearly this figure varies according to income, family size, and Scrooge Factor, but two rules of thumb apply here. First, set yourself a budget for each gift and

---

57 By this stage, he is likely to be making about as much sense as she did too, and, depending on the length of the run to the shops, the possibility of pea-green projectile vomiting cannot be discounted.

work within that budget. Second, try and be as equitable as possible not just among the people for whom you buy but also with regard to those who buy for you. Giving one child a much more expensive present than another is a surefire recipe for trouble; so too is giving someone a present whose price bears no resemblance to that of the present they bought you, irrespective of which way the disparity goes.

An Amazon gift voucher doesn't exactly scream 'I have sweated blood to find the right present for you.'

When to buy

The earlier in the run-up to Christmas the better, if only for your stress levels. Black Friday may provide decent savings on larger and more expensive items, but for most presents it will make little or no difference. If you're going shopping in the real world rather than simply online, go earlier in the morning when the shops will be emptier. In a department store with a central escalator between the floors, start at the top and work down: you'll see more of the floor below as you descend the escalator towards it, and may spot an item or two which you wouldn't necessarily have considered.[58]

---

58 Don't channel the spirit of Father Ted and get stuck in the lingerie department. Especially if you're a priest.

How to choose

If you don't know what someone wants, there are worse ideas than either going very old (retro, vintage) or very new (technology). Failing that, think of something you enjoyed receiving and see whether something similar would be good for them. Any present which shows you've put time and thought into it will be appreciated, irrespective of whether you get it quite right or not. An Amazon gift voucher is all well and good, and may indeed be what they want, but it doesn't exactly scream 'I have sweated blood to find the right present for you.' Stores like the Danish chain Flying Tiger (often just 'Tiger' in the UK, where they have almost 100 stores) are great for stocking fillers, offering a huge selection of things which are fun, quirky and cheap.[59]

How to wrap presents

Measure the paper before wrapping, or simply wrap it round the present before cutting. There should be only a 1cm or so overlap on each edge: too much extra paper looks messy. Ribbons are very useful for covering up mishaps. If the present is oddly shaped, put it in a pouch or a box before wrapping. When attaching a card to the top of a wrapped present, take a small length of sellotape, loop it on itself with the adhesive side facing outwards, and then use that to attach the underside of the envelope to the wrapping paper. Make sure the

---

59 Bluffer's is not on commission from Flying Tiger, more's the pity. The chain's cheap-and-cheerful ethos can be seen in its name: the Danish pronunciation of 'tiger' sounds a lot like 'tier', their word for 'ten', and in the first stores in Denmark in the mid-1990s all items cost 10 kroner.

wrapping paper you use is neither too thin (and can therefore tear easily) or too thick (and therefore difficult to mould or shape). If possible, find wrapping paper which the recipient will notice and love.

When to open presents

There's no hard and fast rule, and every family does things differently. Most households open presents sometime in the 24 hours between late afternoon on Christmas Eve and late afternoon on Christmas Day.[60] Whenever you choose to do so, make sure that:

- children and the elderly open theirs first – the children because they'll explode with excitement if they don't, the elderly because it's all too easy for them to feel left out
- children hand out one present for each one they receive
- someone has a pen and paper to write down who's received what so the correct thank-you letters can be written later
- everyone looks thrilled to receive each present, whether they are or not. When it comes to disappointment, honesty is the best policy only if the giver isn't there with you in person and you can be sure that your reaction will never get back to them

---

60 The Royal Family open all of their presents on Christmas Eve, over dinner. Then again, they can't really do it after lunch on Christmas Day as the Queen has to go and talk to the nation at exactly 3pm, which must be really annoying for her when all she wants to do is slump on the sofa guzzling Quality Street.

- and that there's a large refuse sack to hand to clear up all the discarded paper.

Returning and regifting

You thought the present minefield ended the moment all presents have been opened? Ha! The bluffer knows that this is, if not exactly the start, at least the interval before extra time.

In terms of etiquette (as opposed to statutory consumer rights), and assuming you have the receipt, you can return a present if you know the giver well enough to explain why you're doing so and to be sure they won't be offended. Wrong size or duplicate clothing is always a valid reason.[61] Wrong style is more tricky. If you can't return the item, for whatever reason, then you can regift it further down the line, but again only if you're absolutely sure that the original giver will never find out. And whatever you do, don't regift it back to that original giver. Yes, it's happened. Many times.

No presents

There are growing movements to opt out of buying Christmas presents altogether, or to ask people to donate to good causes in lieu. Some of these movements are part of a more general 'buy-nothing' minimalist anti-consumerist stance, when people eschew all spending other than absolute necessities; others are specifically

---

61 From the giver's point of view, if you don't know someone's size, err on the small side. Someone size 12 will be much happier returning a size 8 than a size 16.

applicable to Christmas, or at least begin at Christmas when people baulk at the scale of spending expected from them. This is harder to exercise when small children are involved, and even those who do follow a minimalist Christmas often make an exception for children (perhaps by making gifts for them rather than buying them).

Adherents of such movements say they feel liberated by stepping off the treadmill. 'When I thought back to past Christmases,' one is quoted as saying, 'I realised I couldn't remember what I got, but I could remember where I was and who I was with. Now, instead of stressing about buying presents, I place more importance on relaxation and family time and I look forward to Christmas much more.' This noble position isn't quite so clever when the non-giver discovers that he/she's the only member of the gathering who subscribes to the no-present scenario.

FESTIVE FARE

ON the Eighth Day of Christmas, gifts received to date from True Love:

8 maids a-milking,
14 swans a-swimming,
18 geese a-laying,
20 gold rings,
20 calling birds,
18 French hens,
14 turtle doves, and
8 partridges in a pear tree.

The average Briton consumes around 7,000 calories on Christmas Day, according to the *Daily Mirror*. (Recommended daily intakes are 2,500 for men and 2,000 for women. Tour de France cyclists can consume up to 9,000 per day, but you burn more off cycling up Alpe d'Huez than you do slumped on the sofa in front of *The Royle Family.* …)

The bluffer is safe in saying that on average, women do not attempt cooking their first Christmas lunch until the age of 34. More than a quarter of men admitted that their partner's lunch is better than their mother's, though whether they told this just to the person conducting the survey or to the mother and/or partner as well remains unclear. The strain of cooking saw the chef take their first sip of Christmas Day alcohol at 11.48am Heck: as the song goes, it's five o'clock somewhere.

TURKEY

Play word association with the phrase 'Christmas food', and the first answer you'll get is almost always 'turkey'. Though some people eat turkey all year round, it's usually much less popular than chicken, beef or lamb: but every year in Britain ten million turkeys are sold in December alone. It's not a good time to be a turkey.

However good turkey tastes as the centrepiece of Christmas lunch it tastes ten times better three days later, especially when combined with ham in a sandwich which could do double duty as a doorstop.

It wasn't always this way. In the Middle Ages, roast boar was the main course of choice (very much shades of Asterix and Obelix); in the 16th and 17th centuries it was goose or capon, and perhaps peacock or swan if you were rich.[62] Turkey was by no means unknown – Henry VIII was known to have had it for Christmas[63] – but goose remained the most popular dish up until Victorian times.

Working-class families would make contributions to a 'Goose Club', allowing them to save up for a year and afford a Christmas goose. The desirability of turkey is shown in *A Christmas Carol*, when Scrooge sends Bob Cratchitt a large turkey to replace the goose Cratchitt had intended to eat.

However good turkey tastes as the centrepiece of Christmas lunch, it tastes ten times better as part of leftovers three days later, especially when combined with ham, brown bread and butter in a sandwich which could do double duty as a doorstop. Fact.

CHRISTMAS PUDDING

According to the *Independent*, Britons spend almost £50m each year on Christmas pudding, also known as plum pudding. The bluffer will, of course, know that the pudding does not contain any plums, and will also know that the reason it was called 'plum pudding' was that 'plum' was an old-fashioned word for 'raisin'. The pudding is traditionally composed of 13 ingredients

---

62 The bluffer can muse here on how changing times and mores alter what is and isn't seen as acceptable to eat.

63 Probably as an hors d'oeuvre, judging from the size of him.

to symbolise Jesus and his 12 apostles, though this is perhaps slightly illogical: the meal with which they are most synonymous took place at Easter rather than Christmas.[64] These ingredients can include dried fruits, egg, suet, treacle, cinnamon, nutmeg, cloves, ginger, and so on.

The pudding can be aged for anything between a month and a year, with its high alcohol content[65] ensuring that it doesn't spoil. Its long cooking time, plus the dark sugars and perhaps dark beers in it too, help contribute to its near-black colouring. The tradition of putting small silver coins in the pudding which could be kept by the person whose serving included them came from the superstition that this would bring wealth in the coming year; it was not exclusive to Christmas and dates back many centuries (coins were often placed in cakes too).

One of the earliest plum pudding recipes is given by Mary Kettilby in her 1714 book *A Collection of above Three Hundred Receipts in Cookery, Physick and Surgery*, which brings to mind a half-delicious, half-alarming image of Mary happily making her pud while on the adjacent table a surgeon is cheerfully performing an anaesthetic-free amputation on some poor soul chewing a Christmas tree.

Christmas pudding used to be cooked and served immediately (it never needed an oven, which made it

---

64 Depending on the chef's levels of sensitivity, volatility and alcohol consumption, it may well be your Last Supper too if you criticise the pudding too heavily.

65 Yes, yes, like everyone else in the house at Christmas. These gags write themselves sometimes, they really do.

popular among working-class families who tended not to possess one), but now it is reheated on the day, either by steaming or that well-known ancient method of the microwave. Brandy heated in a spoon until it burns with a blue flame is poured over it, a custom which again goes back at least as far as Dickens. 'Mrs Cratchit entered – flushed, but smiling proudly – with the pudding, like a speckled cannon-ball, so hard and firm, blazing in half of half-a-quarter of ignited brandy, and bedight with Christmas holly stuck into the top.'

And then it's eaten with – well, take your pick. Brandy butter, cream, ice cream, custard. All of the above, if you really want to go for it, and since it's Christmas you *should* really want to go for it, no?

BRUSSELS SPROUTS

Another of those foodstuffs which seem only to see the light of day for one month in every 12, but is actually big business: the *Daily Express* says that the UK's brussels sprouts industry is worth £650 million. The bluffer will know that the sprout is indeed a 'Brussels sprout' rather than a 'brussel sprout', and it's so named for the most obvious of reasons, that it was cultivated in Belgium during the Middle Ages.[66] Brussels sprouts as a Christmas dish first appear in Eliza Acton's 1845 *Modern*

---

66 Rumours that Brussels sprouts are the vanguard of some ghastly EU plot to standardise Christmas across the entire EU (see *The Bluffer's Guide to Brexit*) are unfounded. Also, not to be confused with the Jolly Green Giant's sidekick Little Green Sprout, former speedway rider Sprouts Elder, or 1980s band Prefab Sprout.

Cookery for Private Families (the same book which mentions 'Christmas pudding' for the first time, curiously). They are popular at Christmas because they grow in the winter and taste better after a frost: the ice sweetens them.[67] The world record for sprout consumption is 31 in a minute by Sweden's Linus Urbanec in November 2008. His friends almost certainly remained upwind of him until at least Christmas Day that year.

MINCE PIES

Also originally known as Christmas pies or crib pies, as their shape was supposed to resemble Jesus's cradle in the stable (they were more oblong then than they are now). They also used to be savoury rather than sweet (hence the 'mince', usually from mutton and flavoured with spices), and the change only really began in the 18th century when Britain began to import sugar from slave plantations in the West Indies.

CLEMENTINES

Obligatory at Christmas, not just for the smell but also because you need some Vitamin C, dammit. And, no, a Terry's Chocolate Orange does *not* contain sufficient quantities.

---

67 The good news for sprout-haters is that global warming will therefore clearly put an end to the sprout trade sooner rather than later. The bad news is that sprouts can be grown hydroponically in vast polytunnels.

QUALITY STREET

The great thing about Quality Street is (a) the unevenness of tastes in any given household and (b) the fact that nature, or at least internet-based retail sites, abhors a vacuum. Therefore there will always be the ones which are scoffed in the first half-hour of opening the tin, and the ones which are still hanging around, unloved, unwanted and uneaten, come the New Year. In the author's house, the first category comprises the coconut ones (so much so that he and his wife compete to have some SAS-style mission as to who can secure most without the other realising) and the second comprises the orange and strawberry ones. The author's mother has solved the Coconut Conundrum by finding, buying and sending bags filled purely with coconut Quality Streets. Tim Berners-Lee, we love you.

PIGS IN BLANKETS

Sausages wrapped in bacon. Meat wrapped in meat. Say no more.

EGGNOG

More an American drink than a British one, but not unknown in Blighty (and in fact originated from the medieval English concoction called 'posset' which was used as a remedy for cold and flu). Made from egg whites, milk or cream, sugar, vanilla, nutmeg and at least one alcoholic spirit: in other words, basically an alcoholic custard. Splendidly, US cadets took part in the Eggnog Riot at the US Naval Academy in West Point on 24–25 December 1826, named after a drunken Christmas Day party fuelled by the potent eggy grog. Even more splendidly, Jefferson Davis and Robert E. Lee, who would both play huge parts on the Confederate side during the US Civil War 35 years later, were both present (though neither were charged with any offence). As with many sweet drinks (such as Moscow Mule), the sweetness can mask the amount of alcohol: jazz composer Charles Mingus's eggnog recipe contained enough alcohol, including 151-proof rum, to, in his own words, 'put down an elephant'.

CRACKERS

No Christmas lunch is complete without crackers, which are themselves not complete without party hats, terrible jokes and some absurd game involving slotting a ball bearing through a hole inside a plastic box which will last at best 22 seconds before (a) breaking or (b) being swallowed by the nearest dog or child.

Crackers are – you guessed it – a Victorian invention, credited to confectioner Tom Smith who wanted his packaging to crackle in the way a real fire does. They were originally called 'cosaques' after the tendency of Cossack soldiers to fire their guns in the air.[68]

---

68 And perhaps also because drunken Christmas dancing looks a little like Cossack dancing, albeit (a) unintentionally, (b) only if you squint or (c) not for long until the reveller loses their balance and goes face first into the brandy butter.

CHRISTMAS CULTURE

ON the Ninth Day of Christmas, gifts received to date from True Love:

9 ladies dancing,
16 maids a-milking,
21 swans a-swimming,
24 geese a-laying,
25 gold rings,
24 calling birds,
21 French hens,
16 turtle doves,
9 partridges in a pear tree.

ON THE BOX

The Queen's Speech

(Not to be confused with *The King's Speech*, which was about (a) her dad or (b) a wartime broadcast.) More accurately, it's 'The Queen's Christmas Message'; even more accurately, and certainly more formally, 'Her Majesty's Most Gracious Speech'. It's one of the few instances when the monarch speaks publicly without advice from any government ministers.

The message[69] was first broadcast on radio by her grandfather George V in 1932, and was the idea of John Reith, the BBC's founder. The King was introduced on air by Walton Handy, a 65-year-old local shepherd.[70] Edward VIII never made a broadcast – he acceded to the throne on 20 January 1936 and abdicated on 11 December the same year.[71] His brother and successor, George VI, had a debilitating stammer which was the subject of the Oscar-winning movie *The King's Speech*.

The Queen gave her first message in 1952. The first televised broadcast was five years later. She has done one every year apart from 1969, and that was because the documentary film *Royal Family* had been made that summer to mark Prince Charles's investiture as Prince of Wales. The broadcast was produced exclusively by the BBC until 1996, after which it alternated with ITN (and, since 2011, with Sky as well).[72]

---

69 Not to be confused with 'The Message', the seminal 1982 rap track by Grandmaster Flash and the Furious Five. It's unlikely that Her Maj has, for example, ever opined that 'it's like a jungle sometimes, it makes me wonder how I keep from going under', or bemoaned her inability to see (a) the game or (b) the Sugar Ray fight.

70 Almost certainly not watching his flock by night as, you know, December. *See* Chapter 1.

71 Anyone would think he didn't like Christmas or something.

72 Each message is specially written, of course, though you may be forgiven for thinking that she says pretty much the same thing each year, perhaps even exactly the same thing: 'Sorry chaps, ran out of time to write something, here's the transcript from 1961, let's just go with that, no one will notice.' Best-man speeches aside, surely no one has a higher percentage of drunks in their audience than the Queen at 3pm on Christmas Day.

The marquee Christmas advert

These always follow exactly the same rules:

- Friendship with animals or snowmen?
  ☐ Check.
- Slowed-down stripped-back faux-indie version of famous song covered by the *chanteuse du jour*?
  ☐ Check.
- Subtle but unmistakeable advertising for supermarket chain almost certainly hammering their own suppliers' margins down to as near zero as possible and that's not very Christmassy is it?
  ☐ Check.
- More snow than the Antarctic even though it's set in the Home Counties which sees a white Christmas on average about once every two and a half centuries?
  ☐ Check.
- E-mails from your friends linking to the advert and saying 'OMG THIS IS AMAZING YOU'LL CRY!'
  ☐ Check.

Christmas specials of popular TV shows

Usually filmed in August and therefore a triumph of the thespian art to pull off the tinsel-and-party-hat look when it's 30 degrees outside and all the crew off-camera are in shorts and T-shirts. Closely related: 'event' TV dramas to run over two or three nights in the dog days between Christmas and New Year. Most recently, adaptations (rather good ones, too) of Agatha Christie novels such as *And Then There Were None*. People forced into a house together, tension, murderous intent, wild accusations and mutual suspicion – it's a perfect reflection of Christmas, let's face it.

HARDY PERENNIAL CHRISTMAS FILMS

A flying snowman in, er, *The Snowman*. A flying car in *Chitty Chitty Bang Bang*. Lots of cars and Michael Caine in *The Italian Job*. Not many cars but lots of Michael Caine and quite a few British soldiers in *Zulu*. Quite a few British soldiers in *Escape to Victory*, and quite a few Nazis too. Quite a few Nazis in *The Sound of Music*, and some nuns too. A German bloke (but not a Nazi) played by a British bloke in *Die Hard*, and some businessmen too. And a nasty businessman in *It's a Wonderful Life*, as Christmassy a film as *The Snowman* itself.

Talking of *Die Hard*, there's a vigorous debate[73] as to whether or not it's a Christmas film or just one which happens to be set at Christmas. The bluffer should always argue that it is a Christmas film, because deconstructing popular culture with deadpan intellectual seriousness is very much a bluffer's *raison d'etre*, *modus operandi*, and any other fancy phrase in a foreign language you care to mention.

To bolster his case, the bluffer should allude to the following points:

- like Joseph, John McClane is a weary traveller[74]
- that McClane just wants to be with his wife Holly at Christmas
- that Holly's called Holly, for heaven's sake

---

73 I.e. a few people on the internet with nothing better to do.

74 Never mind the trek from Nazareth to Bethlehem in the middle of winter, that JFK–LAX route can be murder.

- that McClane is stuck in a confined space with people he wants to kill and who want to kill him. In other words, everyone's Christmas
- that, like Mary, Holly's colleague is pregnant
- that gold, frankincense and myrrh more or less equate to $640m in untraceable bearer bonds, once you've adjusted for inflation etc.

CHRISTMAS MUSIC

Drunken and sentimental, full of anger and resentment but also hope and love, 'A Fairytale of New York' is the perfect Christmas song.

During the Cold War, it is widely believed that the CIA would use Christmas music as part of their resistance-to-interrogation training. (Even if this example of dark arts is unsubstantiated, it's worth a bluff.) If an agent could listen to 'I Believe in Father Christmas' and 'Rockin' Around the Christmas Tree' on an endless loop for 48 hours, they figured, a stint of KGB torture would seem like a walk in the park by comparison. 'Yuri, we will never break this Americanski. Listen to him. He says he will deck the halls with boughs of holly.'

When it comes to Christmas songs, you have to start with 'A Fairytale of New York' by The Pogues and

Kirsty McColl. Drunken and sentimental, full of anger and resentment but also hope and love, it's the perfect Christmas song. Shane MacGowan and McColl spark off each other so well, and if you don't shed a tear either during the soaring chorus about the boys of the NYPD choir singing 'Galway Bay' or the moment when McGowan sings 'can't make it all alone, I've built my dreams around you', check your pulse, as you may already have gone to the great Christmas tree in the sky.

The bluffer will know several things about 'A Fairytale of New York' and, given that it's the most played Christmas song of the 21st century in the UK, will have plenty of opportunity to drop these baubles of festive knowledge:

- It never reached number 1. It was beaten to top spot by the Pet Shop Boys' version of 'Always on My Mind' in 1987, the year it was released.[75]
- It was named after J.P. Donleavy's 1973 novel 'A Fairy Tale of New York', which McGowan's bandmate Jem Finer was reading at the time and had left lying around the studio.
- MacGowan wrote most of the lyrics during a bout of double pneumonia in Malmö, Sweden. 'You get a lot of delirium and stuff, so I got quite a few good images out of that,' he said.
- MacGowan and McColl recorded their vocals

---

75 As such, of course, it's in good company. Other iconic songs which only ever reached number 2 include Ultravox's 'Vienna', Don McLean's 'American Pie', The Kinks's 'Waterloo Sunset', 'Wonderwall' by Oasis, 'Last Christmas' by Wham! and 'Let It Be' by the Beatles.

separately, although they appeared together on *Top of the Pops* and in the song's promotional video.

- Despite the line 'the boys of the NYPD choir still singing "Galway Bay"', the NYPD (New York City Police Department) does not have a choir.
- In the video, MacGowan's playing at a piano while McColl sings, but the hands in the close-up shots aren't his: they're those of another bandmate, James Fearnley, wearing MacGowan's rings on his fingers.
- Also in the video, the police officer who arrests MacGowan and takes him to the cells is played by the American actor Matt Dillon.

The best-selling Christmas song of all time is, of course, Irving Berlin's 'White Christmas', which has sold more than 100 million copies: 50 million of Bing Crosby's version and 50 million by other singers combined.[76] Both La Quinta Hotel in Hollywood and the Arizona Biltmore in Phoenix claim that Berlin was staying in their hotel when he wrote the song, and legend has it that when he finished he told his secretary, 'I just wrote the best song I've ever written – heck, I just wrote the best song that anybody's ever written!'

Crosby's first public performance was on Christmas Day 1941, a few weeks after Pearl Harbor, and the Armed Forces Network was flooded with requests for

---

76 For Christmas to be officially classified as 'white' in England, a single snowflake needs to be observed falling in the 24 hours of 25 December on the roof of the Met Office HQ in London. The odds of this happening are 1 in 10.

the song. The first official master recording was made in May 1942, but it was used so frequently over the next five years that Crosby had to make another recording in March 1947. It's this latter version which is most often heard these days. Crosby himself played down his role, saying that 'a jackdaw with a cleft palate could have sung it successfully'.

'I just wrote the best song I've ever written – heck, I just wrote the best song that anybody's ever written!'
Irving Berlin on 'White Christmas'

The best-selling Christmas single in Britain is 1984's 'Do They Know It's Christmas?' by Band Aid, written in response to the famine in Ethiopia that year. Apart from knowing that Sting sings the line 'the bitter sting of tears', the bluffer will also be able to answer the questions posited in the song and/or point out the various factual errors therein:

- since 60% of Ethiopians are Orthodox, Protestant or Catholic, it's fairly safe to assume that they do, in fact, know it's Christmas
- the line 'there won't be snow in Africa this Christmastime' is untrue: Mount Kilimanjaro has a permanent snowcap at the summit and also receives fresh snowfall every November and December

- the line 'the only water flowing is the bitter sting of tears' is also untrue. The Congo river alone discharges at 41,000 cubic metres a second into the Atlantic, many times greater than the combined discharge of all British rivers.[77]

'Do They Know It's Christmas?' kept Wham!'s 'Last Christmas' off number 1. 'Last Christmas' is the highest-selling single in British history never to have reached top spot, and the video was the last time George Michael was filmed without a beard.

---

[77] The bluffer may at this point concede that he's taking all this a little too seriously.

The Christian meaning of Christmas has been superseded by rampant commercialisation, with 'Christmas creep' seeming to begin a little earlier every year.

SOCIAL RAMIFICATIONS

ON the Tenth Day of Christmas, gifts received to date from True Love:

10 lords a-leaping,
18 ladies dancing,
24 maids a-milking,
28 swans a-swimming,
30 geese a-laying,
30 gold rings,
28 calling birds,
24 French hens,
20 turtle doves,
10 partridges in a pear tree.

It's axiomatic both that 'Christmas isn't what it used to be' and that 'the true spirit of Christmas has been lost'. Both these statements, one way or another, end up back at the same point: that in an increasingly secular society, the Christian meaning of Christmas has been superseded by rampant commercialisation, with 'Christmas creep' seeming to begin a little earlier every year until, to quote the American TV presenter Jon Stewart, 'it looks like Santa's balls have exploded'.

Where the bluffer can excel is by putting some meat on the bones of this contention, particularly with regard to some judiciously dropped facts and figures. Is Christmas a good or bad thing for the economy? The bluffer can argue it both ways.[78]

SANTANOMICS

A good thing:

Many industries ramp up production and sales in the lead-up to Christmas. Toys[79] and books, for instance, are both examples of items bought in disproportionate amounts at Christmas. Moreover, the American tradition of massive shopping days on Black Friday (the fourth Friday of November, the day after Thanksgiving) and Cyber Monday three days later has recently come over to the UK, and is likely only to increase. Discounted but still relatively expensive tech items are especially big sellers at this time.

In 2018, UK shoppers spent £19.2bn during various

---

78 Indeed, the bluffer should argue it both ways, depending on how others in the conversation are leaning. The art of bluffing is also the art of Knowing Which Way the Wind Is Blowing.

79 On average, two-thirds of toy companies' annual sales occur in the final quarter of the year. This affects not only sales figures but also product development cycles: about 80% of a company's products will be new in any given year, and a new product takes between 12 and 18 months to develop.

retail sales in the year to mid-November, and then £7.7bn over the Black Friday/Cyber Monday weekend alone; that is, more than a quarter of the annual total to that point in one (extended) weekend. Though this has to some extent impinged on the traditional Boxing Day and January sales, they too are still important in terms of retail.

Between 10% and a third of gifts by value is a waste, or what economists call 'deadweight loss'.

This extra spending, of course, means an increase in employment to cope: not just in retail stores and firms which provide courier services,[80] but also restaurants and bars too.[81] In fact, spending increases in almost every consumer-related industry in the run-up to Christmas. As a result, companies grow their profits and workers have extra cash to spend. For students in particular with debt to pay off and ability to work in their vacations, seasonal work like this can be

---

80 Certain online retail outlets, including one which may or may not (a) share its name with a large South American river or (b) have exceptionally skilful employees minimising its tax liabilities, often use individual couriers delivering parcels in their own cars alongside regular, uniformed firms.

81 Two words for you: office parties. Two more words for you, repeated: the horror! The horror!

extremely useful. The Birmingham Christmas Market[82] brings £85 million to the city, not just through sales but also through stallholders renting accommodation in the city for up to two months.

Much of Christmas spending is, in one way or another, wasteful. When people buy presents 'blind' for each other, they risk the fact that the recipient will neither want nor need the item. Economist Joel Waldfogel calculates that 'between 10% and a third of gifts by value is a waste, or what economists call 'deadweight loss'.[83] In the UK, an estimated £700m worth of gifts are unwanted. But this doesn't have to be a negative thing. Unwanted presents are often resold online, thus generating two extra phases of economic activity (the sale and the use to which the vendor puts the extra cash).

SCROOGENOMICS
A bad thing:
Outside of consumer-related industries, Christmas may be a time of decreased rather than increased productivity. An average employee may find themselves attending not just one but several Christmas parties – a departmental one, a wider company one, perhaps the ones of their biggest clients and/or suppliers too. Add to these personal parties (people tend to get together more

---

82 Itself an idea imported from Germany: *see* Chapter 11.
83 This loss is the difference between what the gift-giver spent on the item and what the gift receiver would have paid for the item.

before Christmas), hangovers, distractions and so on, and it's no surprise that even the most eager of beavers may find their motivation flagging.[84]

Increasingly, too, companies – especially small ones – seem to be extending the Christmas break into the New Year: it's no longer uncommon for such companies to shut down a day or two before Christmas and only reopen a few days into the New Year, a break of between 10 and 14 days. And Christmas Day itself is almost a total wipeout in terms of consumer spend: few businesses open and few people venture to the shops other than for absolute essentials.[85]

> When it comes to dealing with snowfall, the UK is totally, almost hilariously, inept. A light dusting of snow can bring more or less the entire country to a halt.

Another factor which can impact on the 'Christmastime' economy is extreme weather. When it comes to dealing with snowfall, the UK is totally, almost hilariously, inept. A light dusting of snow can bring

---

84 Not actual beavers, obviously. They show no let-up in activity throughout the colder months, choosing neither to hibernate nor migrate.
85 Under the terms of the Christmas Day (Trading) Act 2004, shops over 280m²/3,000sq.ft are prohibited from opening on Christmas Day in England and Wales.

more or less the entire country to a halt, with disruption to transport and the consequent effect on workers, trade and deliveries running to costs in the hundreds of millions.[86]

No matter how economically active people are during December, there's often an equal and opposite reaction in January, when belts are tightened (both literally and metaphorically). People go out less, they buy less, they drink less. And since they have often paid for some or all of the festive season on credit cards or overdrafts, they are now paying these off, or not as the case may be – and unpaid credit cards, as any economist will tell you, are not a healthy economic sign but quite the opposite. The bigger the bubble, the more likely it is to burst.

THE PARADOX OF THRIFT

If there was no obligation to give Christmas presents, more people might invest their money in the stock market, or in savings accounts, or pay down their

---

86 The enterprising bluffer can, of course, use such circumstances to attempt to make some extra money of their own, by offering odds on any or all of the following appearing on the news:

   Hatchback spinning its wheels impotently in snow

   Unfeasibly cheery driver saying 'nightmare, innit?' while being interviewed through car window

   Drone shots of snowbound motorway tailbacks

   Harassed police officer in hi-viz jacket asking people not to travel 'unless absolutely necessary'

   Shots of airport and/or railway departure boards all saying 'CANCELLED'

   Footage of crowds at airports looking tired and frustrated

   Small child sledging on tea tray.

mortgages, which would in turn allow banks to invest in new businesses. The advantage of this would work both ways: individuals and families with less debt would have more buying power. This is an example of the paradox of thrift.[87]

A healthy economy generates Christmas spending by giving us extra money to spend, not the other way around. And the bluffer can argue that skewing economic activity so much according to a particular time of year is not especially helpful. Spending is good for the economy no matter when it happens, and actually it makes it easier for everyone the less it fluctuates – easier for employers to budget and employees, especially casual or freelance ones, to secure regular income.

Environmentally speaking, Christmas definitely has a negative effect (the planting of Christmas trees notwithstanding). Transporting goods, manufacturing decorations, unwanted gifts, excessive packaging and uneaten food all contribute to the fact that the immediate Christmas period accounts for 5.5% of the

---

[87] The paradox of thrift is prime bluffer territory. Put simply, the paradox states that an increase in individual saving leads to a decrease in aggregate demand, which in turn leads to a decrease in gross output, which in turn leads to a decrease in total savings. Having dropped this in, the bluffer can then go on to airily mention the 'fallacy of composition', by which an assumption concerning one part of a situation is extended to cover all parts: for example, no atoms are alive, therefore nothing made from atoms can be alive. The paradox was first stated in Bernard Mandeville's 1714 *The Fable of the Bees*, and was later popularised by Adam Smith and John Maynard Keynes. Confused? Not as much as your interlocutors will be, and though they may have heard of Smith and Keynes, they will almost certainly not have heard of Mandeville (which has nothing to do with a mandible).

UK's annual carbon dioxide emissions, not to mention 30% more rubbish than usual.[88]

Sadly, Christmas is also a good time for divorce lawyers. The first Monday back to work in the New Year resounds to the ping of e-mails into the inboxes of said legal eagles from wives and husbands for whom the tension of Christmas together was the last straw. Good for legal fees, sure, but bad for everyone else.

---

[88] The amount of wrapping paper used and discarded every year could stretch to the moon if each sheet was laid end-to-end. Give or take a roll or two.

AROUND THE WORLD

> **ON the Eleventh Day of Christmas, gifts received to date from True Love:**
>
> 11 pipers piping,
> 20 lords a-leaping,
> 27 ladies dancing,
> 32 maids a-milking,
> 35 swans a-swimming,
> 36 geese a-laying,
> 35 gold rings,
> 32 calling birds,
> 27 French hens,
> 20 turtle doves,
> 11 partridges in a pear tree.

The bluffer is by definition a well-travelled soul, if that definition refers to the bluffing rather than the travelling. A few judicious references to how Christmas is celebrated in certain countries, an oblique hinting that this knowledge is from personal experience (but never actually saying so in as many words, of course. That would be lying. The bluffer does not lie. The liar lies. The bluffer bluffs.)

As with Nine Lessons and Carols, here are nine countries on whose Christmas traditions the bluffer can expound.

AUSTRIA

Apart from the Christmas markets (*see* Germany: Austria has them too), Austria's Christmas can boast the Krampus: half-goat and half-demon. The Krampus is

---

Austria's Christmas can boast the Krampus: half-goat and half-demon. The Krampus is hairy (usually brown or black), with a goat's horns and cloven hooves and a demon's long tongue and fangs.

---

hairy (usually brown or black), with a goat's horns and cloven hooves and a demon's long tongue and fangs. He carries chains (which he thrashes around), bells and birch branches,[89] and he roams the streets looking for naughty children to punish.

---

89 The chains are thought to represent the Church's binding of the devil, and the birch branches are probably a pagan holdover. As for the bells – well, they give a bit of atmosphere, don't they?

The Krampus is very much the anti-Santa: where Santa rewards the good kids and ignores the bad, the Krampus goes one step further. Sometimes he just frightens children; sometimes he bundles them up in his sack for drowning, eating or taking to Hell.[90] In the first week of Advent, and particularly on the night before St Nicholas's Day (6 December), young men dress up as the Krampus and go out in public. It's called the Krampuslauf (Krampus run).

It sounds terrifying, frankly. No wonder the tradition was banned in the 1920s and, though resurrected after the war, discouraged again in the 1950s (the government distributed pamphlets titled 'Krampus Is an Evil Man'.

COLOMBIA

Christmas in Colombia really begins on 7 December with the Day of the Candles (Día de las Velitas), when candles and paper lanterns are *everywhere* in honour of the Immaculate Conception the next day. Streets

---

90 Yes, very reminiscent of the Child Catcher in *Chitty Chitty Bang Bang*. Not that he gave a generation of children nightmares or anything. Fun fact: Robert Helpmann who played the Child Catcher, was a trained ballet dancer, an ability which was credited with making his movements so sinister. Talking of *Chitty Chitty Bang Bang*, the bluffer will also know that the screenplay was written by Roald Dahl from a book by Ian Fleming, the second time Dahl had adapted a Fleming book after his script for *You Only Live Twice*. The bluffer might also hold forth on the similarities between *Chitty Chitty Bang Bang* and a typical Bond film, beginning with the Child Catcher as megalomaniacal villain and also including: eccentric inventor (Caractacus Potts/Q); woman with innuendo-laden name (Truly Scrumptious/take your pick); and car which transforms into a boat (the titular Chitty Chitty Bang Bang/*The Spy Who Loved Me*).

are turned into tunnels of light and competitions for the best displays are keenly contested. The city of Medellín is particularly well known for its displays, and the festival has also had unexpected side-effects: in 2010, the government erected lights in jungle trees which lit up when anti-government guerrillas passed by, illuminating banners asking them to lay down their arms. More than 300 guerrillas did so.

GERMANY

The novelty of the Christmas market is slightly wearing off now they're becoming an established part of Christmas in the UK, but Germany still has the biggest and the best (with the arguable exception of Birmingham, which even has a singing moose called Chris). Christmas markets are huge business. Four million people visit Cologne's market every year, ahead of Dortmund (3.5m), Frankfurt and Stuttgart (3m) and Dresden and Nuremberg (2m).

They began in the Middle Ages: Dresden has had one since 1434, Frankfurt since 1393 and Munich since 1310.[91] The markets usually run for the four weeks of Advent, and are most often held in the main square of a town, and include not just gifts but food, drink, singing and dancing.[92] Some markets have a local child acting out the part of Jesus as a boy on their opening night.

---

91 The mack daddy (ask your children) of them all, however, is Vienna (1294).

92 Mostly planned and executed by professionals. Occasionally more amateur and impromptu when Uncle Horst has had one stein too many.

Mastering the German language and its compound nouns is, naturally, an integral part of the bluffer's armoury ('mastering', of course, in its lesser-used sense of 'learning the relevant words, the entirety of the relevant words, and nothing but the relevant words'). The following are all Christmas market catnip.

- Christkindlmarkt
- Christkindlesmarkt
- Christkindlmarket
- Christkindlimarkt
- and – just to be different – Weihnachtsmarkt.

All the above are different words for the market itself.[93] Here's what you might find in them.

- Eierpunsch (version of eggnog)
- Gebrannte mandeln (candied, toasted almonds)
- Glühwein, hot mulled wine (tastes like adhesive)
- Lebkuchen and Magenbrot (soft gingerbread cookies)
- Nussknacker (carved Nutcrackers)
- Zwetschgenmännle (figures made of decorated dried plums).

ICELAND

Each of the 13 days which end on Christmas Eve is marked by the arrival of one of the Yule Lads. The Yule

---

93 Yes, there is very much a Monty Python-style Judean People's Front/ People's Front of Judea thing going on.

Lads are, according to folklore, the sons of the trolls[94] Gryla and Leppaludi, respectively a child-eating giantess and a lazy slob who stays at home in their cave all day. Be honest, who hasn't had neighbours like that?

Each of the Yule Lads arrives in turn, causes a specific type of mischief according to their name and proclivity for being annoying, and then leaves after 13 days (so the last one departs on Epiphany, to coincide with the end of the 12 Days of Christmas as we understand it). The Lads line up as follows:

Icelandic name	English translation	Description	Arrives	Leaves
Stekkjarstaur	Sheep-cote Clod	Harasses sheep, but his stiff peg-legs impede him somewhat	12/12	25/12
Giljagaur	Gully Gawk	Hides in gullies, waiting for the chance to steal milk from a cowshed	13/12	26/12
Stúfur	Stubby	Very short. Steals pans to eat the crust of food left on them	14/12	27/12
Þvörusleikir	Spoon-licker	Steals and licks wooden spoons. Is very thin (not really surprising given his diet)	15/12	28/12
Pottaskefill	Pot-scraper	Scrapes leftovers from pots and eats them	16/12	29/12
Askasleikir	Bowl-licker	Hides under beds and steals bowls	17/12	30/12

94 As in genuine folklore monster who lives in rocks/under bridges, not as in person who sits on their laptop all day making deliberately provocative statements online to wind people up.

Icelandic name	English translation	Description	Arrives	Leaves
Hurðaskellir	Door-slammer	Slams doors, especially in the night to wake people up	18/12	31/12
Skyrgámur	Skyr-gobbler	Loves *skyr* (Icelandic yogurt)	19/12	1/1
Bjúgnakrækir	Sausage-swiper	Hides in the rafters and swipes sausages being smoked beneath him	20/12	2/1
Gluggagægir	Window-peeper	Peeps through windows looking for things to steal	21/12	3/1
Gáttaþefur	Doorway-sniffer	Uses outsize nose and sense of smell to locate bread	22/12	4/1
Ketkrókur	Meat-hook	Steals meat using a hook	23/12	5/1
Kertasníkir	Candle-stealer	Steals candles from children	24/12	6/1

On each of the 13 nights the Yule Lads are due to arrive, children place shoes by the window. If they've been good, they get a present; if they haven't, they get a rotten potato. Thirteen nights of present/no-present dichotomy tend to concentrate children's minds on behaving well! (If they don't, of course, the Yule Lad can deliver a rotten potato for that day alone, which is slightly less traumatic than the traditional Santa system with its all-or-nothing annual judgement on Christmas Eve.)

Icelanders are also known to serve roast reindeer at Christmas. Rumours that Rudolf and his eight chums have unilaterally declared the country a no-fly zone remain unconfirmed.

JAPAN

Christmas in Japan means KFC. Yes, you heard that right, and yes, KFC is exactly what you think it is – Kentucky Fried Chicken. More to the point, if you want to be sure of getting a table you need to book way in advance, as every KFC branch is running at full capacity on Christmas Day (some of them take up to ten times their usual daily revenue, and Christmas packages account for a third of KFC Japan's annual turnover).

The link between Christmas and KFC in Japan goes back to 1970 and, for those who despair at the commercialisation of it all, this is yet another example. Takeshi Okawara, manager of Japan's first KFC restaurant, overheard some foreigners talking about how they missed having turkey for Christmas, so he came up (in a dream, as legend has it) with the idea of a 'Party Barrel' – a red-and-white barrel filled with chicken – as a substitute.

Four years later, KFC rolled this out nationally as part of an expanded marketing plan called 'Kentucky for Christmas' ('Kurisumasu ni wa kentakkii' in Japanese). It soon became insanely popular, and nowadays more than 3.5m Japanese celebrate Christmas with KFC meals alongside wine, champagne and Christmas cake.[95] It's not just families who do this, either: Christmas at KFC is also a romantic occasion for couples in a similar way to Valentine's Day.

---

95 The Harvard-educated Okawara wasn't unrecognised for his part in all this: he was promoted through the ranks all the way to the top, serving as president and CEO of KFC Japan between 1984 and 2002.

Christmas in Japan means Kentucky Fried Chicken. More than 3.5 million Japanese celebrate Christmas with KFC meals alongside wine, champagne and Christmas cake.

Christmas isn't a holiday in Japan, and only 1% of the population are Christian, so in some ways KFC had the pitch to themselves. The campaign has been widely held up as a model for advertising and marketing businesses. 'It filled a void,' said Joonas Rokka, associate professor of marketing at Emlyon Business School in France. 'There was no tradition of Christmas in Japan, and so KFC came in and said, this is what you should do on Christmas.' This was aided by the fact that Japan is a society which reveres its elders, and so dressing up the benevolent white-haired Colonel Sanders as the equally benevolent white-bearded Santa Claus was always going to be a winner.

THE PHILIPPINES

The city of San Fernando styles itself as the 'Christmas Capital of the Philippines',[96] and on the Saturday before

---

96 Not sure how much actual competition there is for this title. Could be hotly contested. Could be every other city in the Philippines going 'Yeah, San Fernando, knock yourselves out.'

Christmas Eve it hosts the Giant Lantern Festival (the especially confident bluffer will refer to it in the original language, of course: *Ligligan Parul Sampernandu*). The general idea is that eleven *barangays* (villages) try to build the most elaborate *parol* (lantern). In this respect San Fernando has much in common with Medellín, Colombia, in the lantern stakes.

The *parol* is traditionally made from bamboo and paper and shaped like a star[97] with two tails, and the first one was made in 1908. Their use was practical as well as decorative, allowing rural worshippers to find their way to dawn Masses in areas without electricity. The lanterns in the festival are, of course, larger and more ambitious, using a variety of materials (including shells, glass, beads, wood and metal) and often extravagantly designed with more tails and points than are traditional; some of the more complex shapes include roses, snowflakes, sea urchins, bromeliads,[98] and traditional Western Christmas tropes too (Santa, reindeer, trees etc.) Some can be more than 10m across.

The *parol* is perhaps best described as the Filipino version of the Christmas tree: the ubiquitous and easily understood symbol of the season. (The similarities extend to the fact that both are traditionally taken down

---

97 To symbolise the Star of Bethlehem, the victory of light over darkness, and hope and goodwill.

98 This last one is especially good to drop into gatherings where no gardeners or horticulturalists are present, as then you may well be asked what a bromeliad is and therefore qualify for double bluffer points. And if you're feeling especially confident say that the lantern shapes have occasionally been inspired by Imelda Marcos's shoes.

on or before Epiphany.) To this extent, they are also popular among expat Filipino communities in cities like Vienna, Chicago, San Francisco and Los Angeles.

POLAND

Christmas Eve in Poland is, like the proverbial football match, a game of two halves: a day of fasting, a night of feasting. The feast is known as Wigilia ('The Vigil') and only begins when the first star in the sky has been spotted (in memory of the Star of Bethlehem, of course), The task of spotting the star is delegated to young children, of course.

At the meal itself, pieces of hay and money are placed beneath the tablecloth: the first as a reminder of Christ's birth in a manger, the second as a wish for good fortune and prosperity in the coming year. Wigilia begins with the breaking of the *opłatek*, the Christmas wafer: everyone eats a piece as a symbol of their unity with Christ. An extra place is set in many homes in case a stranger or an angel should appear, and the dinner traditionally contains 12 dishes, one for each of Jesus's apostles. These dishes usually include carp, beetroot soup, meatless ravioli, potato salad and pickled herring. Polish cuisine is very much an acquired taste.

SWEDEN

At the start of Advent in 1966, a 13m-tall three-tonne traditional figure of a Yule Goat made from straw over a wooden skeleton was built in the city of Gävle's Castle

Square. On New Year's Eve, an arsonist burned it down. Since then, both have become traditions – the building of the Gävle Goat and the burning it down (or at least attempting to). The goat has been damaged in 37 of the 53 years it's been erected, despite security measures (not just personnel but chemical treatment and/or soaking it in water to give a coating of ice) and the presence of a fire station nearby. If the goat's burned down before 13 December, it's rebuilt that year; if after that date, it's left until the following year.

A top-ten timeline highlights of the Gävle Goat:

- 1970: two drunk teenagers burn it down six hours after it's built.
- 1988: English bookmakers offer odds on the goat being burned. It survives.
- 1993: the Swedish Home Guard are deployed to watch over the goat. It survives.
- 1996: 24/7 camera surveillance is introduced.
- 1998: the goat is burned down during a blizzard when security guards are sheltering inside. They survive.
- 2001: the goat is burned down by a man from Ohio whose defence is that he thought it was a legal, sanctioned tradition. He spends 18 days in jail.
- 2004: the goat's homepage is hacked into and one of the two official webcams changed.
- 2005: the goat is burned by vandals dressed as Santa and the Gingerbread Man. The hunt for the arsonists is featured on Swedish TV3's 'Most Wanted' (*Efterlyst*) programme.

- 2006: the goat is fireproofed with Fiber ProTector Fireproof, as used in aeroplanes.
- 2015: Police arrest a man fleeing the scene with a singed face, holding a lighter and smelling of gasoline. He admits to being drunk and calls it 'an extremely bad idea'.

VENEZUELA

Worshippers heading for Christmas morning services in Caracas often go on roller skates or rollerblades[99] – a tradition so popular that many roads are closed to cars until 8am. In similar vein, smaller towns or city neighbourhoods hold *patinatas* festivals where adults sing, eat and drink while children play with skateboards, rollerblades and bicycles.

---

99 The bluffer will, of course, know the difference. Roller skates have wheels at or near the corners of the foot: rollerblades have wheels in a line down the centre.

The first rule of Christmas: just survive it. Aim no higher than that. Enjoyment is a bonus. Survival is paramount.

SURVIVAL GUIDE

ON the Twelfth Day of Christmas, gifts received to date from True Love:

12 drummers drumming,
22 pipers piping,
30 lords a-leaping,
36 ladies dancing,
40 maids a-milking,
42 swans a-swimming,
42 geese a-laying,
40 gold rings,
36 calling birds,
30 French hens,
22 turtle doves, and
12 partridges in a pear tree.

Total number of gifts received from True Love, 364 (one for very nearly every day of the year). See Glossary for estimated value of this.

You're going to need a bigger tree, aren't you?

CHRISTMAS SURVIVAL TIPS

Like *Fight Club*, Christmas has two rules. The first rule of Christmas: just survive it. Aim no higher than that. Enjoyment is a bonus. Survival is paramount.

The second rule of Christmas: see first rule.

The bluffer can always drop in some basic survival tips according to the simplest mnemonic of all: the word 'C-H-R-I-S-T-M-A-S' itself.

Children

There's a lot of truth to the old adage that happy children make happy parents, and never more so than at Christmas. Seeing the joy and wonder on children's faces can melt the heart of the stoniest Scrooge and the grumpiest Grinch; but sulks, tantrums and other childish bad behaviour[100] can ruin things just as quickly.

Children need three things: entertainment, exercise and food. And they need presents. Obvs. Teenagers are old enough to take responsibility for all these things themselves (whether they do or not is a different matter), but younger children require more careful planning. Board games, family movies and activities with grandparents who are staying can take up time. Treasure hunts are a good way of combining both exercise and entertainment.

Getting them running around (the children, not the grandparents) is crucial. Getting them out of the house if

---

100 It goes without saying that childish bad behaviour is often not confined to children.

possible (for a walk in the afternoon, that is, not locked out all night, tempting though it may be) to let off some steam is also crucial. And just as crucial as either of these two very crucial things is ensuring that heavy exercise does not follow directly on from mealtimes. ...

Uncle Luke isn't the one dealing with the sugar rush and the hurricane-force tantrums when it all kicks off, is he? No, he isn't.

Bedtimes shouldn't be altered too much, but allowing them to go to bed slightly later than usual is no bad thing – it'll hopefully find the sweet spot between making sure they're tired when they do go to bed, but not so overtired that they have a meltdown. A slightly later bedtime also helps emphasise that this time of year is different and a bit special.

As ever, start winding them down an hour or so beforehand. They might all love Uncle Luke who comes to stay once a year and plays wild games with them, but Uncle Luke isn't the one dealing with the sugar rush and the hurricane-force tantrums when it all kicks off, is he? No, he isn't. Uncle Luke's still downstairs with the vintage port whistling 'It Wasn't Me' by Shaggy. On Christmas Eve, remind them that Santa won't come till they're asleep.[101]

---

101 May not work on teenagers.

Children are very sensitive to unfair treatment. This is particularly important if you have a blended family with children who may be half- or step-siblings to each other. Make sure you treat all children the same, even if you think your own offspring are 24-carat angels and those of your partner would be a shoe-in for lead roles in any reboot of *The Omen* franchise. Try to put yourself in the shoes of the children themselves and imagine how they would feel in any given situation.

Help

There's always a lot of stuff to do at Christmas, and that stuff doesn't get done by itself. A little help goes a long way. Very few cooks will say no to an extra pair of hands in the kitchen (though be sensitive of their egos and/ or feelings too: kitchens are territorial zones and many cooks like to do it their way and only their way). If you're not great with cooking, there are plenty of other things you can be doing.

Washing-up will never go unappreciated, for a start.[102] Laying the table. Putting the rubbish out. Cleaning the house. Walking the dog. Slumped in a comfortable chair all day being waited on hand and foot might work for Jim Royle and Roman emperors, but is unlikely to work for you, at least not indefinitely. Sooner or later, slobs will get things thrown over them rather than handed to them.

---

102 There's something quite therapeutic about washing-up in any case, especially when done in water so hot you can feel it through your Marigolds. No? Just me, then.

> Two FTSE 100 chief executives can easily end up wrestling over the TV remote control and shouting 'Mum! Make him give it back!'

Relax

If you feel your stress levels rising – and you almost certainly will at some stage – do your best to disengage. Take a few deep breaths, find some space of your own for a few minutes, and calm down. Is what's bothering you really all that important? Do you really need to watch that particular programme (especially now everything's available on demand/catch-up anyway)? Does it really matter that Grandpa is taking ages to play his turn in Monopoly or Charades?

It's just one day, maybe two or three, and then it's over. It'll go off much more quickly and easily if you don't try to bend every minute of it to your will. Even the most difficult guest is just that – a guest. And soon they will be gone. Unless it gets really bad (as in really, really bad, as in DEFCON 1 bad), just grin and bear it.

Remember that every family has one weird relative. If you don't know who it is, look in the mirror. And it doesn't matter how old you are or how high-powered your job is: when you and your siblings reassemble under your childhood roof, you will instantly revert to your childhood roles. Two FTSE 100 chief executives can easily end up wrestling over the TV remote control and shouting 'Mum! Make him give it back!' Don't be those people. As they sing in *Frozen*, let it go.

Immunity

Not from prosecution (though that may be useful if things really do go wrong and you end up in court, but let's not get ahead of ourselves here), but from what you know are your normal trigger points. Similar to the previous point about relaxation, but more particularly about things you know in advance will wind you up – specifically, what certain family members are bound to say or do at some stage over Christmas. You can't change who they are, but you can control how you react to them.

Your mother telling you that you spoil your children? Smile sweetly and change the subject. Your teenage son lecturing the adults about climate change? Smile sweetly and change the subject. Your great-uncle launching into a borderline racist rant? Smile sweetly and change the subject. Your mother-in-law giving you cold cream for ageing skin? Thank her profusely and put it in the drawer for presents to recycle on to someone else.[103] When a great-aunt you haven't seen for 20 years says 'My, how you've grown!' the correct response is NOT 'My, how you've aged.' In the words of Michelle Obama: 'When they go low, we go high.' Be like Michelle. And whatever you do, whoever you're with, remember the most important four words of all:

---

103 Probably back to her next Christmas, the mean old witch.

Do
Not
Mention
Brexit.

Social

Unless you are the most extrovert personality around, and/or permanently on MDMA, ration your socialising. The run-up to Christmas can be as exhausting as Christmas itself, and the latter will be a lot less enjoyable than it might be (or even less enjoyable than it usually is, depending on your attitude/standards) if you go into it knackered and grouchy. You don't need to go to every party out there. Most people, unless they're very close friends, won't even notice that you're not at their party.[104] Sorry to break it to you, but they really won't.

Travel

If possible, make people come to you rather than vice versa. Christmas travel is a nightmare whichever way you cut it; there's a reason Santa takes the aerial route during the noise-pollution no-fly-zone times. Motorways are packed day and night as everyone's had the same 'let's beat the rush' idea you have; train services are up the swanny, down the wazoo and round the bend due to some genius's idea to start Massive Engineering Works on 21 December; and as for airports, let's just say that if budget airlines had been around in Dante's day he'd

---

104 And if they do, it'll be the next morning and you can just blame it on their drunken amnesia.

have given his hell ten circles rather than nine. With any luck the relatives you're looking forward to seeing least will get stuck in a tailback so enormous that it warps space and time, and they'll end up spending Christmas either in a black hole or at the Days Inn at Fleet Services on the M3 (doubles from £49).

Money
Budget well in advance for presents and other expenditure. Christmas is – or should be – a time to step away from the hurly-burly of everyday life for a few days, and it's hard to do that if you're worried sick that all your credit cards are maxed out.

Air
Literally and metaphorically, you need air over Christmas. Getting everyone out for a walk is a good, perhaps a vital, antidote to everyone going stir crazy and getting cabin fever. If you like to exercise, don't just stop over Christmas. Try going for a run or doing a workout first thing in the morning: it'll energise you for the day ahead, it'll mean you won't run out of time or inclination to do it later, and it'll help clear any head soreness from the previous night. That's the idea anyway.

Solo
With so many people around a confined space, sometimes you need some time on your own. Make sure to take any such opportunities. Think of being alone in the same way that hostages and soldiers are advised to eat and sleep whenever they have the chance in case it

doesn't come again for a long time. So too here. This also applies to couples, who may find they have little or no time for each other over the festive period. Even going out for an hour to get a coffee together is better than nothing.

The impact of being alone is, of course, reversed if you really are spending Christmas alone. At a time when everyone else is with people, it can be extremely lonely and debilitating (or perhaps extremely enjoyable and liberating). If you do feel down at Christmas singledom, enforced or otherwise, try as far as possible to treat it as though it's just another day.

Log off all social media. You know deep down that behind those shiny happy Instagram feeds are Chernobyl-style explosions, but you won't quite be able to convince yourself of that. If friends invite you round for Christmas lunch, go. Perhaps volunteer at a homeless shelter or similar (the concourse of Euston station is sometimes used for mass charity lunches on Christmas Day, and those who go to help often say that they find it genuinely uplifting).

There's no point in pretending that you know everything about Christmas – nobody does (including the author). But if you've got this far and absorbed at least a modicum of the information and advice contained within these pages, then you will almost certainly know more than 99% of the rest of the human race about the most popular feast day on the Christian Calendar, how to prepare for it, how to enjoy it, and how to survive it. Most importantly you will know how to pretend to know more about it than you do. What you now do with this information is up to you, but here's a suggestion: be confident about your new-found knowledge, see how far it takes you, but, above all, have fun using it. You are now a fully fledged expert in one of humankind's most valued and unique traditions – the offering of peace and goodwill to all men and women, children, and animals (unless you're a turkey).

And if you remember just one piece of advice, frequently repeated throughout these pages, it is this: extend the gifts of cordiality and hospitality to all your friends and family, don't run out of food or drink (especially Quality Street), and don't harbour dark thoughts about plying the assembled gathering with powerful sedatives so that you can steal a few well-deserved private moments of festive cheer and tranquility.

GLOSSARY

Advent. Latin word meaning 'coming' which begins four Sundays before Christmas. Coincidentally, also the exact period during which small children can maintain peak excitement.

Angels. Constituents of heavenly choir which sings at Christmastime. Also Robbie Williams song which, despite only ever reaching number 4, was voted the best single of 1980–2005 and is now the song most Britons want played at their funeral.

Blitzen. One of Santa's reindeer. Also an exclamation of surprise.

Boxing Day. 26 December. Named after the tradition of employers giving servants and tradespeople a 'Christmas Box' on the day after Christmas Day. Also description of what happens in pub car parks up and down the country when everyone's had a bit too much to drink and someone accuses someone else of looking at him/looking at his bird/spilling his pint/all the above.

Chestnuts. But only roasting on an open fire.

Chimney. A hollow structure allowing smoke from an indoor fireplace to vent outside. Preferred method of Santa's ingress to and egress from domestic dwelling-places. How his red suit is never stained black, and his beard never on fire, is not explained.

Christmas Carol, A. Dickens novel which did much to shape modern-day perceptions of Christmas. Also, the bane of the life of every woman called Carol over the festive period because yes, mate, she's heard all the jokes before.

Christmas jumper. An unholy abomination. A harbinger of the apocalypse. Owned by 82% of the population, according to a Matalan survey, with more than 75% of those wearing them to a work event and more than half also sporting one on Christmas Day. We, as a society, are doomed.

Cinnamon. A spice obtained from tree bark. Pervasive scent not just of Christmas but also high street coffee chains' cappuccinos.

Comet. One of Santa's reindeer. A defunct electrical retail chain which went bust just before Christmas 2012. If you still have a gift token, don't count on it.

Cracker. A festive explosive device containing a novelty gift of limited value or interest; also how Uncle Leslie describes every female under 70.

Cupid. One of Santa's reindeer. Roman god of desire and erotic love. Odd name for a reindeer, which are lovely, but not noticeably objects of desire unless you're another reindeer, or in Lapland where they're on menus everywhere.

Dancer. One of Santa's reindeer. When prefixed with 'exotic', euphemism for performer in gentlemen's clubs (in this instance, 'gentlemen' is also something of a euphemism).

Dasher. One of Santa's reindeer. Of arguable interest is that it is also the name of a Romanian car manufacturer spelt DACIA, which makes 'Duster' SUVs and is owned by Renault.

Die Hard. Best Christmas film ever. Fact. Proves the inalienable truth that British male actors make the best screen villains. In this case it was the late and much lamented Alan Rickman who, as ever, stole the show.

Donner. One of Santa's reindeer. Not to be confused with: Donna Summer; doner kebab; the French verb to give.

Epiphany. Feast day celebrated on 6 January, commemorating the Magi's visit to the baby Jesus.

Also used to describe a sudden revelation, e.g. that you hate your entire family at around 4pm on Christmas Day.

Frankincense. Aromatic resin used in perfumes. Not to be confused with any of the following Franks: Lampard, Lloyd Wright, N. Furter, Rijkaard, Spencer, Sinatra, Skinner (not the comedian's real name, which bluffers will know is Chris Collins).

Frosty. Snowman with corncob pipe, button nose and eyes made out of coal. Brought to life by magical silk hat. A jolly happy soul. Not keen on prolonged sunlight. Not to be confused with: singular sugar-coated corn flake popularised by Tony the Tiger.

Fruitcake. Cake made with dried fruit, nuts and spices. Also, your great-aunt Mabel who's gone a bit funny in her old age.

Goodwill. Sentiment of which you are entirely devoid come Boxing Day.

Goose. Alternative to turkey at Christmas lunch. Tom Cruise's mate who's killed in *Top Gun* when he tries to eject from a flat spin caused by flying through Iceman's jetwash. Every cloud . . .

Grinch. Green, hairy, pot-bellied, pear-shaped Dr Seuss character who absolutely hates Christmas. Patron saint of festive misanthropes everywhere.

Holly. Evergreen flowering plant with prickly leaves, very much associated with Christmas. Not to be confused with: Buddy, Golightly, Willoughby.

Lord of Misrule. Medieval leader of Christmastime celebrations. Now turns up at the House of Lords now and then, nods off during debates, wakes with a startled 'Eh? What? Claret? Yes, yes, absolutely', and toddles off for a spot of lunch.

Miracle. An extraordinary, positive event inexplicable by scientific laws. Also, a Christmas which passes off without any form of disagreement whatsoever.

Partridge. Bird in a pear tree. Also inept broadcaster called Alan who has in the past had an 'A-ha!' catchphrase, a graveyard radio slot on Radio Norwich, a Ukrainian girlfriend and a co-hosting gig on *This Time*.

Prancer. Yet another one of Santa's reindeer. Not to be confused with Dancer.

Presents. How does Darth Vader know what Luke's getting for Christmas? Because he has felt his presents.

Puritans. Prudish English Protestants who banned Christmas for a few years in the 17th century. Many people come Boxing Day wish they'd kept it that way.

Queen's Speech. Annual tradition occasionally featuring footage of the monarch asking people at garden parties if they've come far and hoping that Prince Philip doesn't say anything *too* racist.

Rudolf. Scarlet-schnozzed reindeer, famous for being ostracised by Santa's other reindeer until he is chosen to deploy his magnificent shiny and glowing hooter to safely guide the sleigh through a foggy Christmas Eve. If a bluffer were to be picky, it might make more sense to have him at the back of the sleigh to use his red nose as a brake light.

Snowflake. Not often seen on Christmas Day in the United Kingdom. Also, easily offended millennial.

Stockings. Easy, tiger. Not those kind of stockings. Christmas stockings. Large empty sock-shaped bags (or sometimes pillow-cases) left out for Santa to fill with presents. The tradition is thought to have begun with the original St Nicholas, who threw gold through the window of a poor man who refused to accept charity. The gold landed in a stocking which was hanging drying by the fire.

Tinsel. Invented in 1610 in – you guessed it – Germany. Designed to look like ice, it was originally made from silver strands and is now usually PVC film.

Turkey. Country of 82 million people straddling Europe and Asia. Known by the Romans as 'Anatolia' which, let's face it, sounds a lot better than a large flightless bird of the genus Meleagris. Turkeys are known for having a healthy lifespan of ten years unless they're a bit slow off the mark around Christmas Day and Thanksgiving.

The Twelve Days of Christmas. Equal parts Christmas carol and cumulative song (think 'Ten Green Bottles' and the like); *see* page 58. Enumerates the gift-giving of a lover who is clearly (a) wealthy,[105] (b) resourceful, (c) well-prepared, (d) borderline obsessional and (e) doesn't know when the joke has worn thin.

Vixen. One of Santa's reindeer. Female fox. Quarrelsome and/or sexually voracious woman. (Odd name for a reindeer, which are generally a good-natured migratory species of deer which can travel more than 3,000 miles in a year – unless they're pulling Santa's sleigh, in which case they go a lot further in a single evening.)

---

105 According to PNC financial services, the total costs of the gifts in 2018 would have come out at just over £135,000.

A BIT MORE BLUFFING...